Harmless as Doves

Harmless as Doves

Thomas Watson

Christian Focus Publications

As far as the publishers are aware, the sermons of Thomas Watson included in this volume have been out of print since last century. A minor degree of editing was thought necessary to make the contents suitable for modern readers.

© 1993 Christian Focus Publications Ltd
ISBN 1 85792 029 X

This edition published in 1993 by Christian Focus Publications Ltd
Geanies House, Fearn, Ross-shire, IV20 1TW, Scotland, Great Britain.

Printed and bound in Great Britain by
Cox & Wyman Ltd, Reading, Berks

Cover design by Donna Macleod
Cover photograph by Roy Dennis, Inchdryne, Nethybridge

CONTENTS

1

Christian Prudence and Innocency

'Be ye therefore wise as serpents, and harmless as doves'
(Matthew 10:16).

The apostle saith, 'All scripture is given by inspiration' (2 Timothy 3:16). God's Word is compared to a lamp, for its enlightening quality (Psalm 119:105), and to silver refined, for its enriching quality (Psalm 12:6). Among other parts of sacred writ, this, in the text, is not the least: 'Be ye wise as serpents, and harmless as doves.' This is the speech of our blessed Saviour: his lips were a tree of life which fed many; his works were miracles; his words were oracles, and deserve to be engraved upon our hearts as with the point of a diamond. This is a golden sentence: 'Be ye wise as serpents, and harmless as doves.' Our Lord Jesus, in this chapter, firstly, gives his apostles their commission; secondly, foretells their danger; thirdly, gives them several instructions.

1. Christ gives his apostles their commission
Before they went abroad to preach, Christ ordains them in verse 5: 'These twelve Jesus sent forth.' Those who exercise in the ministerial function must have a lawful call, 'No man takes this honour to himself, but he that is called of God' (Hebrews 5:4). Christ gave not only the apostles and prophets, who were extraordinary ministers, a call to their office but even 'pastors and teachers' (Ephesians 4:11).

But if one has gifts, is not this sufficient to the ministerial office?

No: as grace is not sufficient to make a minister, so neither are gifts; therefore it is observable, that the Scripture puts a difference between gifting and sending, 'How shall they preach unless they be sent?' (Romans 10:15). If gifts were enough to constitute a minister, the apostle should have said, 'How shall they preach unless they be gifted?' But he saith, 'Unless they be sent': which denotes a lawful call, or investiture into the office. The attorney that pleads at the bar may have as good gifts as the judge that sits upon the bench; but he must have a lawful commission before he sits as a judge. If it be thus in matters civil, how much more in church matters, which are of higher concern. Those therefore who usurp the work of the ministry without being solemnly set apart for it, show more pride than zeal, and they can expect no blessing, 'I sent them not, nor commanded them; therefore they shall not profit this people at all, saith the LORD' (Jeremiah 23:32). So much for the first: the apostles' commission; 'These twelve Jesus sent forth.'

2. Christ foretells their danger, 'Behold I send you forth as sheep in the midst of wolves' (v 16).

The apostles were going about a glorious work, but it was an hazardous work for they would meet with enemies fierce and savage like wolves. As all that will live godly in Christ shall meet with sufferings, so commonly Christ's ambassadors encounter the deepest trials. Most of the apostles died by the hands of tyrants: Peter was crucified with his head downwards; Luke the evangelist was executed on an olive tree; John was cast by Domitian into a vessel of scalding oil. Maximinus the emperor - as Eusebius relates - gave charge to his officers, to put none to death but the governors and pastors of the church. The ministers are Christ's *antesignani*, his ensignbearers to carry his colours, therefore they are most shot at; they hold forth this truth, 'I am set for the defence of the gospel' (Philippians 1:17). The Greek word, *cheimai*, alludes to a soldier that is set in the forefront of the battle, and has all the bullets flying about his ears. The minister's work is to part between men and their sins; and this causes opposition. When Paul preached against Diana, all the city was in an uproar (Acts 19). This may stir up prayer for Christ's ministers, that they may be able to withstand the assaults of the enemy (2 Thessalonians 3:2).

3. Christ gives the apostles their instructions, whereof this in the text was one: 'Be ye wise as serpents, and harmless as doves.'
(1) The exhortation, 'Be ye wise'; (2) The simile, 'as serpents'; (3) The qualification of this wisdom - a wisdom mixed with innocency, 'harmless as doves.'

This union of the dove and the serpent is hard to find, 'Who then is a wise and faithful servant?' (Matthew 24:45). On which place, saith St Chrysostom, it is an hard matter to find one faithful and wise. Faithful, there is the dove; wise, there is the serpent: 'tis hard to find both. If one would seek for a faithful man, question-less he may find many; if for a wise man, he may find many; but if he should seek for one both wise and faithful, this is a *rara avis*, hard to find, yet it is possible though not common.

Moses, a man 'learned in all the wisdom of the Egyptians' (Acts 7:22), there was the wisdom of the serpent; and the meekest man alive, 'Now the man Moses was very meek, above all the men which were upon the face of the earth' (Numbers 12:3), there was the innocency of the dove.

Daniel was an excellent person, 'Excellent wisdom is found in thee' (Daniel 5:14), there was the prudence of the serpent; and, 'The presidents and princes sought to find occasion against Daniel, but they could find no occasion nor fault' (Daniel 6:4), behold here the innocency of the dove.

Look on St Paul in Acts 23:6, 'When Paul perceived that the one part were Sadducees, and the other Pharisees, he cried out, I am a Pharisee'; by which speech Paul got all the Pharisees on his side; here was the wisdom of the serpent; and in verse 1, 'I have lived in all good conscience before God unto this day'; here was the innocency of the dove.

How amiable is this, the union of the dove and serpent! The

Scripture joins these two together, 'meekness of wisdom' (James 3:13); wisdom, there is the serpent; meekness, there is the dove. This beautifies a Christian, when he has the serpent's eye in the dove's head. We must have innocency with our wisdom, else our wisdom is but craftiness; and we must have wisdom with our innocency, else our innocency is but weakness. We must have the innocency of the dove, that we may not circumvent others; and we must have the wisdom of the serpent, that others may not circumvent us. We must have the innocency of the dove, that we may not betray the truth; and the wisdom of the serpent, that we may not betray ourselves. In short, religion without policy is too weak to be safe; policy without religion is too subtle to be good. When wisdom and innocency, like Castor and Pollux, appear together, they presage the soul's happiness.

Doctrine: *That Christians must be both wise and innocent.*

I begin with the first, wise: be ye 'wise as serpents'.

1. *I shall speak concerning wisdom in general.*

Solomon saith, 'Wisdom is the principal thing' (Proverbs 4:7). It is better than riches, 'Happy is the man that findeth wisdom; for the merchandise of it is better than the merchandise of silver' (Proverbs 3:13,14). If the mountains were pearl, if every sand of the sea were a diamond, they were not comparable to wisdom. Without wisdom, a person is like a ship without a pilot, in danger to split upon rocks.

Job sets for the encomium and praise of wisdom, 'The price of wisdom is above rubies' (Job 28:13-18). The ruby is a precious stone, transparent, of a red fiery colour. It is reported of one of the kings of India, that he wore a ruby of that bigness and splendour, that he might be seen by it in the dark: but wisdom casts a more sparkling colour than the ruby; it makes us shine as angels. No chain of pearl you wear does so adorn you as wisdom. Wisdom consists chiefly in three things:

(1) Knowledge to discern wherein happiness lies.

(2) Skill to judge what will be the fittest means to conduce to it.

(3) Activity to prosecute those things which will certainly accomplish that end.

So much for wisdom in general.

2. *More particularly: wisdom is variously distinguished.* 'Tis either natural, moral, or theological.

(1) *A natural wisdom*, which is seen in finding out the *arcana naturae*, the secrets of nature. Aristotle was by some of the ancients called an eagle fallen from the clouds, because he was of such raised intellectuals, and had so profound an insight into the causes of things. This natural wisdom is adorning, but it is not sufficient to salvation. St Hierom brings in Aristotle with his syllogisms, and Tully with his rhetoric, crying out in hell.

(2) *A moral wisdom*, which consists in two things *malum respuendo,* and *bonum eligendo*. Moral wisdom lies in the rejection of those things which are prejudicial, and the election of those things which are beneficial; this is called prudence. Knowledge without prudence may do hurt; many a man's wit has undone him, for want of wisdom.

(3) *A theological or sacred wisdom*, which is our knowing of God, who is the supreme and sovereign good. Greece was counted the eye of the world for wisdom and Athens the eye of Greece, but neither of them knew God, 'I found an altar with this inscription, To the unknown God' (Acts 17:23). To know God, in whom is both *verum* and *bonum*, truth and goodness, is the master-piece of wisdom, 'And thou, Solomon my son, know thou the God of thy father' (1 Chronicles 28:9). And this knowledge of God is through Christ; Christ is the glass in which the face of God is seen (Colossians 1:15). And then we know God aright, when we know him not only with a knowledge of speculation, but appropriation as in Psalm 48:14, 'This God is our God.' This knowledge of God is the most sublime wisdom, therefore it is called, 'Wisdom from above' (James 3:17).

3. But to come nearer to the text, and speak of the wisdom of the serpent: 'Be ye wise as serpents.'

But must we in everything be like the serpent?

No: our Saviour meant not that in every thing we should imitate the serpent. I shall show you: (1) wherein we should not be like the serpent; (2) wherein we should be like the serpent.

1. Wherein we should not be like the serpent.

(1) *The serpent eats dust,* 'Dust shall be the serpent's meat' (Isaiah 65:25). It was a curse upon the serpent. Thus we should not be like the serpent, to feed immoderately upon earthly things. It is absurd for him that has an heaven-born soul, capable of communion with God and angels, to eat greedily the serpent's meat; a Christian has better food to feed on - the heavenly manna, the precious promises, the body and blood of Christ. 'Tis counted a miracle to find a diamond in a golden mine; and it is as great a miracle to find Christ, the pearl of price, in an earthly heart.

The lapwing wears a little coronet on its head, yet feeds on dung: to have a crown of profession on the head, yet feed inordinately on these dunghill-comforts, is unworthy of a Christian. What a poor contemptible thing is the world! It cannot fill the heart. If Satan should take a Christian up to the top of the pinnacle, and show him all the kingdoms and glory of the world, what could he show him, but a show, a pleasant delusion?

There is a lawful use God allows of these outward things, but the sin is in the excess. The bee may suck a little honey from the leaf, but put it in a barrel of honey, and it is drowned. The wicked are thus characterized, 'Who mind earthly things' (Philippians 3:19). They are like Saul, 'hid among the stuff.' We should be as eagles flying aloft towards heavens, and not as serpents, creeping upon the earth, and licking the dust.

(2) *The serpent is deceitful.* The serpent uses many shifts, and glides so cunningly, that we cannot trace him. This was one of those four things which wise Agur could not find out, 'the way of a serpent upon a rock' (Proverbs 30:19). 'Tis a deceitful

creature: we should not in this sense be like the serpent, for deceitfulness. Naturally we too much resemble the serpent for fraud and collusion, 'The heart is deceitful above all things' (Jeremiah 17:9).

Firstly, deceit *towards man*: (1) To dissemble friendship - to cover malice with pretences of love - to commend and censure, to flatter and hate - a Judas' kiss, and a Joab's sword - *mel in ore, fel in corde*. (2) To dissemble honesty; to pretend just dealing, yet use false weights.

Secondly, deceit *towards God*: To draw nigh to God with the lips, while the heart is far from him - to serve God, and seek ourselves, to pretend to love God, and yet be in league with sin - we should not in this sense be like the serpent, deceitful, and given to shifts. O be upright! Be what you seem to be! God loves plainness of heart (Psalm 51:6). The plainer the diamond is, the more it sparkles; the plainer the heart is, the more it sparkles in God's eye. What a commendation did Christ give Nathaniel in John 1:47, 'Behold an Israelite indeed, in whom there is no guile.'

(3) *The serpent casts the coat*, but another new coat comes in the room; in this we should not be like the serpent, to cast the coat, to cast off one sin, and another sin as bad come in the room. The drunkard leaves his drunkenness, because it impairs his health, his credit, his purse, and falls to the sin of cozenage; the prodigal leaves his prodigality, and turns usurer; this is as if one disease should leave a man, and he should fall into another as bad - his ague leaves him, and he falls into a consumption. O be not like the serpent, that casts one coat and another comes! This is like him in the gospel, that had one devil go out of him, and seven worse spirits came in the room (Matthew 12:45).

(4) *The serpent is a venomous creature*, it is full of poison (Deuteronomy 32:24). In this be not like the serpent. It is said of wicked men, their poison is like the poison of a serpent (Psalm 58:4). What is this poison? It is the poison of *malice*.

Malice is the devil's picture. Lust makes men brutish, and

malice makes them devilish.

Malice carries in it its own punishment; a malicious man, to hurt another, will injure himself. Quintillian speaks of one who had a garden of flowers, and he poisoned his flowers that his neighbour's bees sucking from them might be poisoned, and die: Oh be not venomous like the serpent! Malice is mental murder; you may kill a man, and never touch him, 'Whosoever hateth his brother is a murderer' (1 John 3:15).

Malice spoils all your good duties; the malicious man defiles his prayer, poisons the sacramental cup - he eats and drinks his own damnation. I have read of one who lived in malice, and being asked how he could say the Lord's Prayer, he answered, 'I leave out those words, As we forgive them that trespass against us.' But St Austin brings in God replying thus to him: 'Because thou dost not say my prayer, therefore I will not hear thine.' The malicious man is not like to enjoy either earth or heaven; not the earth, for the 'meek shall inherit the earth' (Matthew 5:5); nor is he like to enjoy heaven, for God 'will beautify the meek with salvation' (Psalm 149:4); so that the malicious man is cut off both from earth and heaven.

(5) *The serpent is given to hissing*: so it is said of the basilisk. In this be not like the serpent to hiss out reproaches and invectives against the saints and people of God; they are the seed of the serpent that hiss at godliness. The Lord will one day reckon with men for all their hard speeches (Jude 15). Lucian was such an one who did hiss out and scoff against religion; and as a just judgment of God, he was afterwards torn in pieces by dogs.

(6) *The serpent stops her ear*: it is an obstinate deafness, 'They are like the deaf adder, that stoppeth her ear' (Psalm 58:4). In this be not like the serpent, obstinately to stop your ears to the voice of God's Word. While God calls you to repent of sin, be not as the basilisk to stop your ear, 'They refused to hearken, and stopped their ears, that they should not hear' (Zechariah 7:11). The Word announces threatenings against sin; but many, instead of being like the publican, smiting on their breast, are as deaf

adders, stopping their ears. If you shut your ear against God's Word, take heed God does not shut heaven against you; if God cries to you to repent, and you will not hear, when you cry for mercy, God will not hear, 'As he cried and they would not hear, so they cried and I would not hear, saith the LORD of hosts' (Zechariah 7:13).

(7) *The serpent casts her coat, but keeps her sting*: in this sense be not like the serpent, to cast off the outward acts of sin, and keep the love of sin: he whose heart is in love with any sin, is an hypocrite.

A man may forbear sin, yet retain the love of it; he may forbear the act of gross sin, *formidine poenae*, for fear of hell, as a man may forbear a dish he loves, for fear it should bring his disease upon him, the stone or gout.

A man may forsake sin, yet keep the love of sin; he may forsake sin either out of policy or necessity. Firstly, *policy*: vice will impair his health, eclipse his credit, therefore out of policy, he will forsake it; or, secondly, *necessity*: perhaps he can follow the trade of sin no longer - the adulterer is grown old - the prodigal poor - either the purse fails, or the strength.

Thus a man may refrain from the act of sin, yet retain the love of sin; this is like the serpent, which casts her coat, but keeps her sting. O take heed of this! Herein be not like the serpent; remember that saying of Hierom, *gravius est peccatum diligere quam perpretare*; it is worse to love sin than to commit it. A man may commit sin through a temptation, or out of ignorance, and when he knows it to be a sin, he is sorry for it; but he that loves sin, his will is in the sin, and that aggravates it, and is like the dye which makes the wool of a crimson colour.

(8) *Serpents are chased away with sweet perfumes*; the perfume of harts-horn or the sweet odour of the styrax will drive the serpent away. In this be not like the serpent, to be driven away with the sweet perfumes of holiness. Carnal hearts are for things only which delight the senses; they will discourse of news or traffic, here they are in their element; but let a man bring with him

the sweet perfume of religious discourse - let him talk of Christ, or living by faith - this spiritual perfume drives them away. Oh, be not in this like the serpent! How do you think to live with the saints in heaven, that cannot endure their company here? You hate the sweet savour of their ointments, the fragrant perfume of their graces.

(9) *The serpent (as is noted of the stellio, a kind of serpent) does no sooner cast his skin, but he eats it up again*: in this be not like the serpent to forsake sin, and then take it up again, 'It is happened unto them according to the true proverb, The dog is returned to his own vomit again' (2 Peter 2:22). Such were Demas and Julian. Many, after a divorce, espouse their sins again; as if one's ague should leave him a while, and then come out again; the devil seemed to be cast out, but comes the second time: and, the end of that man is worse than his beginning (Luke 11:26), because his sin is greater; he sins knowingly and wilfully, and his damnation will be greater.

(10) *Serpents are great lovers of wine.* Pliny, who writes the natural history, saith, 'If serpents come where wine is, they drink insatiably.' In this be not like the serpent; though the Scripture allows the use of wine (1 Timothy 5:23), yet it forbids the excess 'Be not drunk with wine wherein is excess' (Ephesians 5:18). Be not like the serpent in this 'lovers of wine'.

Because this sin of drunkenness does so abound in this age, I shall enlarge something more on this head. It is said of the old world, 'They did eat, they drank, till the flood came' (Luke 17:27). Drinking is not a sin, but the meaning is they drank to intemperance, they disordered themselves with drink; and God let them have liquor enough, first they were drowned in wine, and then in water.

There is no sin which does more deface God's image than drunkenness; it changes a person, and does even unman him; drunkenness makes him have the throat of a fish, the belly of a swine, and the head of an ass; drunkenness is the shame of nature, the extinguisher of reason, the shipwreck of chastity, and the murder of conscience; drunkenness is hurtful for the body, the cup kills more than the cannon; it causes dropsies, catarrhs, apoplexies; drunkenness fills the eyes with fire, and the legs with water, and turns the body into an hospital; but the greatest hurt is what it does to the soul; excess of wine breeds the worm of conscience.

The drunkard is seldom reclaimed by repentance, and the ground of it is partly, because, by this sin, the senses are so enchanted, reason so impaired, and lust so inflamed; and partly, it is judicial, the drunkard being so besotted with this sin, God saith of him as of Ephraim in Hosea 4:17, 'Ephraim is joined to idols, let him alone'; so, this man is joined to his cups, 'let him alone', let him drown himself in liquor till he scorch himself in fire.

How many woes has God pronounced against this sin! 'Woe to the drunkards of Ephraim!' (Isaiah 28:1). 'Howl ye drinkers of wine!' (Joel 1:5).

Drunkenness excludes a person from heaven, 'Drunkards shall not inherit the kingdom of God' (1 Corinthians 6:10): a man cannot go to heaven reeling.

King Solomon makes an oration full of invectives against this sin, 'Who has woe? Who has contentions? Who has babbling? Who has redness of eyes? They that tarry long at the wine' (Proverbs 23:29, 30). 'Who has contentions?' Drink when abused, breeds quarrels, it causes duels. 'Who has babbling?' When one is in drink, his tongue runs, he will reveal any secrets of his friend. 'Who has redness of eyes?' Redness of eyes comes sometimes from weeping, but too often from drinking; and what is the issue? At last, the wine bites like a serpent, and stings like an adder (verse 32). The wine smiles in the glass, but stings in the conscience.

Drunkenness is a sin against all the ten commandments:

1. Drunkenness casts off the true God, 'Wine takes away the heart' (Hosea 4:11): it takes the heart off from God.

2. It makes the belly a god (Philippians 3:19). To this the

drunkard pours drink-offerings; there is a breach of the second commandment.

3. The drunkard in his cups takes God's name in vain by his oaths.

4. The drunkard makes no difference of day; he is seldom sober on the Sabbath; he on that day worships Bacchus.

5. The drunkard honours neither his natural father nor the magistrate his civil father; he will be intemperate though the laws of the land forbid it.

6. The drunkard commits murder. Alexander killed his friend Clytus when he was drunk, for whom he would have given half his kingdom when he was sober.

7. The drunkard's wine proves lust. Austin calls wine *fomentum libidinis* - the inflamer of lust. *Nunquam ego ebrium castum putavi*; I never did believe a drunken man to be chaste, saith Hierom.

8. The drunkard is a thief; he spends that money upon his drunken lust, which should have been given to charitable uses; so he robs the poor.

9. The drunkard is a slanderer; he cares not, when he is on the ale-bench, how he does defame and belie others; when he has taken his full cups, he is now fit to take a false oath.

10. The drunkard sins against the tenth commandment, for he covets to get another's estate, by circumvention and extortion, that he may be the better able to follow his drunken trade. Thus he sins against the ten commandments.

If this sin of drunkenness be not reformed, I pray God, the sword be not made drunk with blood. And whereas some will go to shift off this sin from themselves, that they are no drunkards, because they have not drunk away their reason and senses - they are not so far gone in drink that they cannot go - he is a drunkard in the Scripture-sense who is 'mighty to drink wine' (Isaiah 5:22). He is a drunkard, saith Solomon, that tarries long at the wine (Proverbs 23:30). He who sits at it from morning to night - that drinks away his precious time, though he does not drink away his reason - he is a drunkard that drinks more than does him good; and that, though he be not himself drunk, yet he makes another drunk, 'Woe to him that gives his neighbour drink, that puttest thy bottle to him, and makest him drunken!' (Habakkuk 2:15).

Oh, I beseech you, be not in this like the serpent, lovers of wine! This I fear is one cause why the Word preached does so little good to many in this city, they drink away sermons; they do as the hunted deer, when it is wounded, it runs to the water and drinks; so, when they have been at a sermon, and the arrows of reproof have wounded their conscience, they run presently, and drink away those convictions; they steep the sermon in wine. The tavern-bell does more hurt than the sermon-bell does good. Thus you have seen wherein we should not be like serpents.

2. Wherein we should be like the serpent, and that is in prudence and wisdom: 'be ye wise as serpents.'
The serpent is a most prudent creature, therefore the devil made use of the serpent to deceive our first parents, because it was such a subtle creature, 'The serpent was more subtle than any beast of the field' (Genesis 3:1). There is a natural wisdom and subtlety in every part of the serpent, and we should labour to imitate them, and be 'wise as serpents'.

(1) *The serpent has a subtlety in his eye, he has a singular sharpness of sight*; therefore among the Grecians, a serpent's eye was a proverbial speech for one of a quick understanding; in this we should be like the serpent. Get the serpent's eye, have a quick insight into the mysteries of the Christian religion. Knowledge is the beauty and ornament of a Christian, 'The prudent are crowned with knowledge' (Proverbs 14:18). Get the serpent's eye, be divinely illuminated. Faith without knowledge is presumption; zeal without knowledge is passion (Proverbs 19:2). Without knowledge, the heart is not good; for one to say he has a good heart, who has no knowledge, is as if one should say he has a good eye, when he has no sight. In this be like the serpent, of a quick understanding.

(2) *The serpent has a prudence and subtlety in his ear;* the serpent will not be deluded with the voice of the charmer, but stops its ear: in this we must be 'wise as serpents' - stop our ears to false teachers who are the devil's charmers.

1. We must stop our ears to Arminian teachers, who place the chief power in the will, as if that were the helm that turns about the soul in conversion, 'Who maketh thee to differ from another?' (1 Corinthians 4:7). *Ego me ipsum discerno*, said Grevinchovius, I have made myself to differ. Be as the serpent, stop your ears to such doctrine.

2. We must stop our ears to Socinian teachers, who raze the foundation of all religion, and deny Christ's divinity. This the apostle calls 'a damnable heresy' (2 Peter 2:1).

3. We must stop our ears to Popish teachers, who teach merit, indulgences, transubstantiation; who teach that the Pope is the head of the church. Christ is called 'the head of the church' (Ephesians 5:23): for the Pope to be head is to make the church monstrous, to have two heads. Popish teachers teach the people nonsense and blasphemy; they cause people to pray without understanding - to obey without reason - to believe without sense; it is a damnable religion; therefore worshipping the beast, and drinking the cup of God's indignation are put together (Revelation 14:9,10).

Oh, in this be 'wise as serpents'; stop your ears to the charming of false teachers! God has given his people this wisdom, to stop their ears to heretics, 'A stranger will they not follow, but will flee from him' (John 10:5).

(3) *The serpent has a chief care to defend his head* - a blow there is deadly: so in this we should be 'wise as serpents'; our chief care should be to defend our head from error. The plague in the head is worst. Loose principles breed loose practices. If the head be tainted with erroneous opinions - that believers are free *a lege morali* - that there is no resurrection - that we may do evil that good may come of it - what sin will not this lead to? Oh keep your head!

Error is a spiritual gangrene (2 Timothy 2:17), which spreads, and if not presently cured, is mortal. Heresies destroy the doctrine of faith, they rend the mantle of the church's peace, and eat out the heart of religion. The Gnostics, as Epiphanius observes, did not only pervert the judgment of their proselytes, but brought them at last to corporal uncleanness: error damns as well as vice. Vice is like killing with a pistol, and error killing with poison. Oh be wise as serpents; defend your head!

'Be ye wise as serpents, and harmless as doves.' Our Saviour Christ here commends to us the wisdom of the serpent, and the innocency of the dove. The elect are called wise virgins (Matthew 25:4); virgins, there is the dove; wise, there is the serpent. We must have innocency with our wisdom, else our wisdom is but craftiness; and we must have wisdom with our innocency, else our innocency is but weakness. We must have the innocency of the dove, that we may not circumvent others; and we must have the wisdom of the serpent, that others may not circumvent us.

This union of the dove and the serpent is hard to find, but it is possible; Moses was learned in all the wisdom of the Egyptians (Acts 7:22); there was the prudence of the serpent; and he was 'meek above all the men which were upon the face of the earth' (Numbers 12:3); there was the innocency of the dove.

But the most famous instance of wisdom and innocency was in our Saviour: when the Jews came to him with an ensnaring question, 'Is it lawful to give tribute to Caesar or not?' (Mark 12:14). Christ answers wisely in verse 17, 'Render to Caesar the things that are Caesar's, and to God the things that are God's' - deny not Caesar his civil right, nor God his religious worship - let your loyalty be mixed with piety; here he showed the wisdom of the serpent. And would you see Christ's innocency? 'There was no guile found in his mouth; who, when he was reviled, reviled not again' (1 Peter 2:22,23) - he opened his mouth in praying for his enemies, but not in reviling them; behold here the innocency of the dove.

The second thing I am to speak of is the dove: 'be harmless as doves.'
The dove is an excellent creature; it was so acceptable, that in the old law, God would have the dove offered in sacrifice. The Holy Ghost, when he would appear in a visible shape, assumed the likeness of a dove (Matthew 3:16). We should be as doves in three respects:

1. *In respect of meekness*
The dove is the emblem of meekness. It is *sine felle*, without gall; we should be as doves for meekness; we must avoid unruly passion, which is *brevis insania*, a short frenzy; we must be without the gall of bitterness and revenge; we must be of mild spirits, praying for our enemies: as did Stephen in Acts 7:60, 'Lord, lay not this sin to their charge.' This dove-like meekness is the best jewel and ornament we can wear, 'The ornament of a meek spirit, which is in the sight of God, of great price' (1 Peter 3:4). Passion does disguise, meekness adorns.

2. *We should be as doves for innocency*
The innocency of the dove is seen in two things:

(a) *Not to deceive.* The dove is, as without gall, so without guile; it does not deceive nor lie at the catch; thus we should be as the dove, without fraud and craft. There is a commendable holy simplicity , 'I would have you simple concerning evil' (Romans 16:19); to be a bungler at sin, not to have the art to beguile, this is a good simplicity; as Nathaniel, in whose spirit there was no guile (John 1:47). Where is this dove-like innocence to be found? We live in an age wherein there are more foxes than doves; persons are full of guile, they study nothing but fallacies, so that one knows not how to deal with them, 'With a double heart do they speak' (Psalm 12:2).

(b) *Not to hurt.* The dove has no horns or talons to hurt, only wings to defend itself by flight; other creatures are commonly well-armed; the lion has its paw, the boar its tusk, the stag its horns, but the dove is a most harmless creature, it has nothing wherewith to offend: thus we should not do wrong to others, but rather suffer wrong. Such a dove was Samuel, 'Whose ox have I taken? or whose ass have I taken? or whom have I defrauded?' (1 Samuel 12:3); he did not get men's estates into his hands, or raise himself upon the ruins of others. How rare is it to find such doves! Surely they are flown away! How many birds of prey are there! 'They all lie in wait for blood, they hunt every man his brother with a net' (Micah 7:2); these are not doves, but vultures; they travail with mischief, and are in pain till they bring forth.

3. *We should be as doves for purity*

The dove is the emblem of purity; it loves the purest air, it feeds on pure grain; the raven feeds on the carcass, but the dove feeds pure. Thus let us be as doves for sanctity, 'Cleansing ourselves from all pollution both of flesh and spirit' (2 Corinthians 7:1). Christ's dove is pure, 'My dove, my undefiled' (Canticles 5:2). Let us keep pure among dregs, 'Keep thyself pure' (1 Timothy 5:22). Better have a rent in the flesh, than a hell in the conscience; the dove is a chaste, pure creature; let us be doves for purity.

Use 1. *See here the nature of a good Christian*

He is wise and innocent; he has so much of the serpent, that he does not forfeit his discretion, and so much of the dove, that he does not defile his conscience. A godly man is looked upon by a carnal eye as weak and indiscreet, as having something of the dove but nothing of the serpent; to believe things not seen, to choose sufferings rather than sin, this is counted folly. But the world is mistaken regarding a believer - he has his eyes in his head - he knows what he does - he is prudent, as well as holy; he is wise that provides for eternity - he is the wisest man that has wit to save his soul - he is wise that makes him his friend who shall be his judge. The godly man acts both the politician and the divine; he retains his ingenuity, yet he does not part with his integrity.

Use 2. Reproof
It reproves them who have too much of the serpent, but nothing of the dove, 'Wise to do evil, but to do good they have no knowledge' (Jeremiah 4:22); these are like the devil, who retains his subtlety, but not his innocency.

(1) We have many in this age like the serpent for craftiness, 'Through his policy also he shall cause craft to prosper' (Daniel 8:25). Men have the head-piece of subtlety, but want the breast-plate of honesty; they are wise to contrive sin, to forge plots, to study compliance, rather than conscience; the port they aim at, is preferment; the compass they sail by, is policy; the pilot that steers them, is Satan. These have the craftiness of the serpent, 'They are wise to do evil.'

(2) They are like the serpent for mischief. You know the fiery serpents did sting Israel: these have a sting in their tongues, stinging the people of God with bitter slanders and invectives, calling them factious and seditious - and they sting with their indictments and excommunications (Galatians 4:29). Such sting-ing serpents were Nero, Diocletian, and Julian; and their spirit is yet alive in the world. These have too much of the serpent in them, but nothing of the dove, 'Their damnation slumbereth not' (2 Peter 2:3).

Use 3. Exhortation
To put in practice our Saviour's counsel in the text, join the serpent and the dove together, wisdom and holiness; here lies the knot - this is the great difficulty - to unite these two together, the serpent and the dove, prudence and innocency; if you separate these two, you spoil all.

Wherein does a Christian join these two together, the serpent and the dove, prudence and holiness?
This I shall answer in twelve particulars.
    1. *To be wise and innocent consists in this, to be sensible of an injury yet not revenge it.* A Christian is not a stoic, nor yet a

fury: he is so wise, that he knows when an injury is done him; but so holy, that he knows how to pass it by. This is a most excellent temper of soul, I had almost said, angelic. As the wind does allay the heat of the air, so grace does allay the heat of revenge. Moses herein showed a mixture of the serpent and the dove: Miriam murmured against him, 'Hath the LORD indeed spoken only by Moses?' (Numbers 12:2). Is he the only prophet to declare God's mind to us? Moses was so wise as to discern her pride and slighting of him; yet so meek as to bury the injury. When God struck her with leprosy, he prays for her in Numbers 12:13, 'Heal her now, O God, I beseech thee.' And upon his prayer, she was cured of her leprosy. A good Christian has so much wisdom as to discern his enemy's malice, but so much grace as to conquer his own; he knows it is the glory of a man to pass by a transgression (Proverbs 19:11). A Christian has so much prudence as to vindicate himself, yet so much goodness as not to avenge himself. Behold here the serpent and the dove united, sagacity and innocency.

2. *The mixing of wisdom and innocency is seen in this, to be humble, but not base.* Humility is part of the dove's innocency, 'Be ye clothed in humility' (1 Peter 5:5). St Paul, though the chief of the apostles, calls himself the least of saints. A gracious soul has low thoughts of himself, and carries himself lowly toward others; but, though he be humble, he is not base; though he will not saucily resist his superiors, he will not sinfully humour them; though he will not do such proud actions as to make his enemies hate him, yet he will not do such sordid actions as to make them despise him; here is the serpent and the dove united.

A good Christian is so humble as to oblige others, but not so unworthy as to disobey God. St Paul, as far as he could with a good conscience, did 'become all things to all, that he might save some' (1 Corinthians 9:20-22); but he would not break a commandment to gratify any. When God's glory lay at stake who more resolute than Paul (Galatians 2:5)? The three children were humble, they gave the king his title of honour, but they were not

sordidly timorous, 'Be it known unto thee, O king, we will not
serve thy gods' (Daniel 3:18). Though they showed reverence to
the king's person, yet no reverence to the image he had set up.

A good Christian will not do any thing below himself; though
he is for obeying of laws, yet he will not prostitute himself to
men's lusts. He is humble - there he shows the innocency of the
dove; but not base - there he shows the wisdom of the serpent.

3. *The prudence of the serpent and innocency of the dove is
seen in this, to reprove the sin, yet love the person.* We are
commanded to reprove: 'Thou shalt not hate thy brother in thy
heart; thou shalt rebuke him, and not suffer sin upon him'
(Leviticus 19:17). Not to reprove sin is to approve it; but this
sword of reproof is a dangerous weapon, if it be not well-handled;
to reprove and yet love is to act both the serpent and the dove.

How may a Christian so reprove sin, as to show love to the
person?

(a) In taking a fit season to reprove another, that is, when his
anger is over. As, when God did rebuke Adam, he came to him,
'in the cool of the day' (Genesis 3:8): so, when we are to reprove
any, we are to come to them when their spirits are more cool and
fit to receive a reproof. To reprove a man when he is in a passion
is to give strong water in a fever; it does more hurt than good. By
observing a fit season, we show both prudence and holiness - we
discover as well discretion as affection.

(b) Reproving sin so as to show love to the person is seen in
this, when, though we tell him plainly of his sin, yet it is in mild,
not provoking words, 'In meekness instructing those that oppose
themselves' (2 Timothy 2:25). Peter tells the Jews plainly of their
sin in crucifying Christ, but uses suasives and gospel-lenitives,
to allure and encourage them to believe, 'Him ye have taken, and
by wicked hands have crucified' (Acts 2:23); 'Repent and be
baptized in the name of Jesus Christ for the remission of sin ... for
the promise is to you, and to your children' (verse 38,39).
Reproof is a bitter pill, and hard to swallow, therefore we must
dip it in sugar; use those sweet mollifying expressions, that

others may see love coming along with the reproof. David compares reproof to oil (Psalm 141:5): oil supples the joints when they are hard and stiff; our reproofs being mixed with the oil of compassion, they work most kindly, and do most soften stiff obdurate hearts.

(c) Reproving sin, yet showing love to the person, is when the end of our reproof is not to revile him but to reclaim him. While we go to heal men's consciences, we must take heed of wounding their names. The chirurgeon, in opening a vein, shows both skill and love - skill in not cutting an artery - and love, in letting out the bad blood; here is the mixing of the serpent and the dove; the wisdom of the serpent is seen, in not reproaching the sinner; the innocency of the dove is seen in reclaiming him from sin.

4. *Prudence and holiness is seen in this, to 'know what we should do, and do what we know'.* To know what we should do - there is the wisdom of the serpent; to do what we know - there is the innocency of the dove (John 13:17). Knowledge is a jewel which adorns him that wears it; it is the enriching and bespangling of the mind; knowledge is the eye of the soul, to guide it in the right way. But this knowledge must be joined with holy practice; to separate practice from knowledge is to separate the dove from the serpent. Many illuminated heads can discourse fluently in matters of religion, but they do not live up to their knowledge; this is to have good eyes, but to have the feet cut off; they know they should not break the Sabbath, they should not defame nor defraud: but they do not practise what they know - here they separate the dove from the serpent, virtue from knowledge. How vain is knowledge without practice! As if one should know a sovereign medicine and not apply it. Satan is a knowing spirit, he has enough of the serpent; but that which makes him a devil is, he wants the dove, he does not practise holiness.

5. *To mix the serpent and the dove, is to keep two trades going.* To understand worldly affairs - there is the wisdom of the serpent; yet not neglect the soul - there is the innocency of the dove. God has said, 'Six days shalt thou labour' (Exodus 20:9). Religion did

never grant a patent to idleness; there is a lawful care to be had
about secular things; to have insight into one's calling is a
commendable wisdom, but with this wisdom join the dove's
innocency; so follow your calling, as not to neglect your soul.
The soul is a precious thing, it would beggar the angels to give
half the price of a soul. Our greatest care should be to get grace.

While you put gold in your bag, do not forget to put oil in your
vessel. Trade beyond the East Indies; drive a trade of holiness.
'This merchandise is better than the merchandise of silver'
(Proverbs 3:14). Live in a calling, but especially live by faith;
look to the providing for your families, but especially to the
saving of your souls. The soul is the angelic part, the loss of this
can never be made up again. Oh unite the serpent and the dove -
prudence and holiness! Use the world, but love your soul; trade
on earth, but beware of breaking in your trade for heaven. How
many part these two, the serpent and the dove? They are wise for
the world, but fools for their souls. It is too often seen, that men
pull down their souls to build up an estate.

6. *To join the serpent and the dove, prudence and innocency,
consists in this, to know how to give counsel, and how to keep
counsel.* He has the wisdom of the serpent that can give counsel;
he knows how to advise another in difficult cases, and speak a
word in due season, 'The counsel of Ahithophel was as if a man
had inquired at the oracle of God' (2 Samuel 16:23). But this is
not enough to have the wisdom of the serpent, in being able to
give counsel; but there must be the innocency of the dove too, in
keeping counsel. If a friend's secret be imparted to us, unless in
case of blood, we are not to reveal it. A friend is *alter idem*, as
one's own soul (Deuteronomy 13:6), and what he imparts of his
heart should be kept under lock and key, 'Discover not a secret
to another, lest he that hear thee put thee to shame,' (Proverbs
25:9,10). To disclose a friend's secret, though it be not treason,
is treachery, and is most unchristian; a word may be spoken in
secret, which, when it is trumpeted out, may occasion quarrels or
lawsuits. He that cannot keep a matter committed to him, is like

a vessel that runs out, or a sick stomach that brings it up again. He that publishes his friend's secret, does publish his own shame.

7. *To mix these two, prudence and holiness, is to know the seasons of grace, and improve them*; to know the seasons of grace - there is the wisdom of the serpent. It is wisdom in the husbandman to know the fit time for pruning of trees, sowing of seed: so it is no less wisdom to know the golden seasons of grace; while we hear the joyful sound - while we have praying hours - while the Spirit of God blows on our hearts - here is a gale for heaven. The day of grace will not always last; the shadows of the evening seem to be stretched out; things look as if the gospel tended speedily to a sun-setting; be wise as serpents, to know what a prize is put in your hands. And with the serpent join the dove, that is, in improving the seasons of grace. The stork and turtle not only know their season but improve it; they approach to the warmer climate against the spring, saith Pliny: here is the serpent and the dove united, knowing and improving the day of grace; when we profit by ordinances - when we mix the word with faith - when an ordinance has stamped holiness upon us, as the seal leaves its print upon the wax - this is to improve the seasons of grace.

8. *The serpent and the dove, wisdom and innocency, is to be moderate yet zealous*. Moderation is good in some cases, 'Let your moderation be known to all' (Philippians 4:5).

(a) Moderation is good in cases of anger. When the passions are up, moderation sits as queen and governess in the soul; it allays the heat of passion. Moderation is *fraenum irae*, the bridle of anger.

(b) Moderation is good in cases of lawsuits; so the Greek word for moderation is properly taken. If there be a dispute in law between us and others, we are not to take the extremity of the law, but use Christian equity and mildness; nay, for peace's sake, *cedere de jure*, rather part with some of our right, than oppress them: this much honours the gospel.

(c) Moderation is good in things indifferent. Things ought not to be rigorously imposed on God's worship which are not of divine injunction. God never made governors of the church to be like pilots of a ship, to steer men's consciences which way they please. Moderation and Christian forbearance, in things indifferent, would much tend to the peace and unity of the church.

All this moderation is commendable, and shows the wisdom of the serpent: but remember to join the dove with the serpent. We must so exercise moderation as withal to cherish zeal. St Paul in some things was moderate: he did not press circumcision (Acts 15:25), he was tender of laying a yoke upon the consciences of the disciples; but he had zeal with his moderation; when he saw the idolatry at Athens, the fire of his zeal broke forth, 'His spirit was stirred in him' (Acts 17:16). It was good advice Calvin gave to Melancthon, that he should not so affect the name of moderate, as to lose all his zeal. To be cool and silent when God's blessed truths are undermined or adulterated, is not moderation but lukewarmness, which is to God a most hateful temper, 'I would thou wert cold or hot' (Revelation 3:15); and anything but lukewarm. This is to show prudence and holiness, when we are moderate, yet zealous.

9. *To unite serpent and dove, consists in this, when we defend the truth by argument and adorn it by life.* Defending the truth is the serpent's wisdom; an intelligent Christian can convince gainsayers. This wisdom of the serpent was eminently in Stephen, 'There arose certain of the synagogue, disputing with Stephen, and they were not able to resist the wisdom and the spirit by which he spake' (Acts 6:9,10). We read in the acts and monuments of the church, of John Fryth, a martyr, being opposed by three papists; he, like another Hercules, fighting with all the three at once, did by his wisdom so convince them, that one of them turned from Popery and became a zealous Protestant. Herein is the wisdom of the serpent, not only to love them that profess the truth, but silence them that oppose it. But with this wisdom of the serpent, there must be joined the innocency of the dove; together with defending the truth by argument, there must be adorning it by life, 'That they may adorn the doctrine of God our Saviour'

(Titus 2:10). There are some who can dispute for the truth, but disgrace it by their bad living; this is to act both the serpent and the dove, when we not only plead for the truth, but walk in the truth, like Nazianzen, of whom it was said, he did thunder in his doctrine, and lighten in his conversation.

10. *The uniting of the serpent and the dove, is to be serious in religion, yet cheerful.* Seriousness puts the heart in an holy frame, it fixes it on God; seriousness is to the soul, as ballast to the ship, it keeps the soul from being overturned with vanity; the heart is ever best when it is serious. But this seriousness in religion must be mixed with cheerfulness; cheerfulness conduceth to health (Proverbs 17:22). It honours religion, it proclaims to the world we serve a good Master; cheerfulness is a friend to grace, it puts the heart in tune to praise God (Psalm 71:21). Uncheerful Christians, like the spies, bring an evil report on the good land: others suspect there is something unpleasant in religion, that they who profess it hang their harps upon the willows, and walk so dejectedly. Be serious, yet cheerful, 'Rejoice in the Lord alway' (Philippians 4:4). Why was Christ anointed but to give the oil of joy for mourning? (Isaiah 61:1-3). Joy is as well a fruit of the Spirit as faith (Galatians 5:22). One way of grieving the Spirit, saith Heinsius, is by Christians' uncheerful walking; if you would render the gospel lovely, mix the dove and the serpent; be serious, yet cheerful in God.

11. *The uniting of the serpent and the dove, wisdom and holiness, consists in this, when we so lay up as we lay out.* It is a duty to provide for our charge, 'If any man provide not for his own, he is worse than an infidel' (1 Timothy 5:8). To lay up for our family - here is the wisdom of the serpent; but we must lay out for the poor too - here is the mixture of the dove, 'Charge them that are rich in the world, that they do good, that they be rich in good works' (1 Timothy 6:17,18). The poor man is as it were an altar, if we bring our alms and lay upon it, with such sacrifices God is well pleased. Faith, though it has sometimes a trembling hand, must not have a withered hand, but must stretch forth itself

to works of mercy; there's nothing lost by charitableness, 'The liberal soul shall be made fat' (Proverbs 11:25); 'Blessed is he that considers the poor, thou wilt make all his bed in his sickness' (Psalm 41:1-3). While men do so remember their family, that they do not forget the poor, they show both prudence and piety; they unite the serpent and the dove.

12. *The serpent's wisdom and the dove's innocency is seen in this - to avoid danger, so as not to commit sin - to preserve our liberty, yet keep our integrity.* There is a sinful escaping danger, namely, when we are called to suffer for the truth, and we decline it; but there is an escaping danger without sin; as thus, when we do not betray ourselves into the enemies' hands by rashness, nor yet betray the truth by cowardice. We have a pattern of this in our Saviour; he avoided his enemies in one place, that he might preach the gospel in another, 'They led him unto the brow of the hill, that they might cast him down headlong; but he passing through the midst of them, went his way' (Luke 4:29,30) - there was Christ's wisdom in not betraying himself to his enemy; and in verse 43, 'I must preach the kingdom of God to other cities also' - there was his holiness. Christ's securing of himself was in order to the preaching of the gospel. This is to mix prudence and innocency, when we so avoid danger as we do not commit sin.

Thus I have, as briefly and as clearly as I could, shown you how we must unite these two, the serpent and the dove, prudence and holiness. For want of coupling these two together religion does much suffer in the Christian world. 'What Christ has joined together, let no man put asunder.' Observe these two, prudence and holiness; here is the serpent's eye in the dove's head. When these two, wisdom and innocency - like Castor and Pollux - appear together, they indicate that much good and happiness will befall a Christian.

On Becoming A New Creature

> Therefore, if any man be in Christ, he is a new creature; old
> things are passed away, behold all things are become new
> (2 Corinthians 5:17).

In this Scripture consists the essence and soul of religion. I note
here two things.

Firstly, *that the true definition of a Christian is to be in Christ*.
'If any man be in Christ.' He may be in the church visible, yet not
in Christ; it is not to be baptized into Christ's name that makes
a true Christian: but to be in Christ, that is to be grafted into him
by faith. And if to be in Christ makes a Christian, then there are
but few Christians. Many are in Christ nominally, not really; they
are in Christ by profession, not by mystical union. Are they in
Christ that do not know him? Are they in Christ who persecute
them that are in Christ? Surely such an holy head as Christ will
disclaim such spurious members.

Secondly, *that whosoever is in Christ, is a new creature*. For
illustration, I shall show, first, what a new creature is; and second,
what kind of work it is.

1. What a new creature is

It is a second birth added to the first (John 3:3). It may be thus
described: it is a supernatural work of God's Spirit, renewing and
transforming the heart into the divine likeness.

(1) *The efficient cause of the new creature, is the Holy Spirit*;
no angel or archangel is able to produce it. Who but God can alter
the hearts of men, and turn stones into flesh? If the new creature
was not produced by the Holy Spirit, then the greatest glory in a

man's conversion would belong to himself; but this glory God will not give to another. The turning of the will to God is from God, 'After I was turned, I repented' (Jeremiah 31:19).

(2) The organical cause or instrument by which the new creature is formed, is the Word of God, 'Of his own will begat he us, by the word of truth' (James 1:18). The Word is the seed, out of which springs the flower of the new creature.

(3) The matter of which the new creature consists is, the restoring of God's image lost by the fall.

But does God in the new creature, give a new soul?

No: he does not bestow new faculties, but new qualities. As in the altering of a lute, the strings are not new, but the tune is mended: so, in the new creature, the substance of the soul is not new, but is new tuned by grace. The heart that before was proud is now humble; the eyes, that before were full of lust, are now full of tears. Here are new qualities infused.

2. What kind of work the new creature is

(1) *The new creature is a work of divine powe*r; so much it imports, because it is a creation. The same power which raised Christ from the grave, goes to the production of the new creature (Ephesians 1:20). It is a work of greater power to produce the new creature than to make a world. It is true, in respect to God, all things are alike possible to him; but, as to our apprehension, it requires a greater power to make a new creature, than to make a world, for,

(a) When God made the world, he met with no opposition; but when God is about to make a new creature, he meets with opposition; Satan opposes him, and the heart opposes him.

(b) It cost God nothing to make the world, but to make the new creature costs him something; Christ himself was constrained to become man. In making the world, it was but speaking a word; but in making the new creature, it cost Christ the shedding of his blood.

(c) God made the world in six days; but he is carrying on the new creature in us all our lives long. The new creature is but begun here, it is not perfected or drawn in all its orient colours till it come to heaven.

(2) *The new creature is a work of free-grace.* There is nothing in us to move God to make us anew; by nature we are full of pollution and enmity, yet now God forms the new creature. Behold the banner of love displayed! The new creature may say, 'By the grace of God I am what I am.' In the creation we may see the strength of God's arm; in the new creature we may see the working of God's bowels. That God should consecrate any heart, and anoint it with grace, is an act of pure love; that he should pluck one out of the state of nature, and not another, must be resolved into free-grace, 'Even so, Father, for so it seemed good in thy sight' (Matthew 11:26). This will increase the saint's triumphs in heaven, that the lot of free-grace should fall upon them, and not on others.

(3) *The new creature is a work of rare excellency.* A natural man is a lump of earth and sin, God loathes him (Zechariah 11:8), but upon the new creature is a spiritual glory, as if we should see a piece of clay turned into a sparkling diamond, 'Who is this that cometh out of the wilderness, like pillars of smoke perfumed with myrrh and frankincense?' (Canticles 3:6). That is the natural man coming out of the wilderness of sin, perfumed with all the graces of the Spirit. The new creature must needs be glorious, for it partakes of the divine nature (2 Peter 1:4). A soul beautified with holiness, is like the firmament bespangled with glittering stars; it is God's lesser heaven (Isaiah 57:15). In the incarnation, God made himself in the image of man - in the new creation, man is made in the image of God. By our being creatures, we are the sons of Adam - by being new creatures, we are the members of Christ. Reason makes one live the life of a man - the new creature makes him live the life of God; a new creature excels the rational nature, and equals the angelic. It is excellent to hear of Christ's being

crucified for us, but more excellent to have Christ formed in us.

Concerning the new creature, I shall lay down two positions. First position: *That it is not in the power of a natural man to convert himself; because it is a new creation. As we cannot make ourselves creatures, so not new creatures.*

But why does God command us to convert ourselves, if we have no power? 'Make you a new heart' (Ezekiel 18:31).

(a) We once had power. God gave us a stock of holiness, but we lost it. If a master gives his servant money to employ in his service, and he wastes and embezzles it, may not the master require his money of him? Though we have lost our power to obey, God has not lost his right to command.

(b) Though men cannot convert themselves, and make themselves new creatures, yet they may do more than they do in a tendency to it; they may avoid temptations, they may read the word; the same feet that carry them to a play will carry them to a sermon; they may implore divine grace. But they do not what they are able; they do not improve the power of nature to the utmost, and put God to the trial whether he will give grace.

(c) God is not wanting to them who seek to him for grace. *Deus volentibus non deest.* He is willing to put to his helping hand. With his command, 'Make you a new heart' (Ezekiel 18:31), there goes a promise, 'A new heart also will I give you' (Ezekiel 36:26).

Second Position: *When God converts a sinner, he does more than use a moral persuasion, for conversion is a new creation,* (Ephesians 4:24).

The Pelagians talk much of free-will; they say, 'The will of man is by nature asleep, and conversion is nothing but the awakening a sinner out of sleep, which is done by moral persuasion.' But man is by nature dead in sin (Ephesians 2:1). And God must do more than awaken him, he must enliven him before he be a new creature.

First Use. Terror to such as are not new creatures.
Such as are still growing upon the stock of old Adam who continue in their sins, and are resolved so to do; these are in the gall of bitterness, and are the most miserable creatures that ever God made, except the devils. These stand in the place where all God's arrows fly; these are the centre where all God's curses meet. An unregenerate person is like one in debt that is in fear to be arrested; he is every hour in fear to be arrested by death, and carried prisoner to hell. Can that traitor be happy, who is fed by his prince in prison, only to be kept alive for execution? God feeds the wicked as prisoners, they are reserved for the day of wrath (2 Peter 2:9). How should this fright men out of their natural condition, and make them restless till they are new creatures.

Second Use. Trial; whether we are new creatures; our salvation depends upon it.

1. I shall show you the counterfeits of the new creature, or that which seems to be the new creature, and is not.

(a) *Natural honesty, moral virtue, prudence, justice, liberality, temperance - these make a glorious show in the eye of the world, but differ as much from the new creature as a meteor from a star.* Morality indeed is commendable, and it were well if there were more of it; this our Saviour loves, 'Then Jesus beholding him, loved him' (Mark 10:21). It was a love of compassion, not election. Morality is but nature at best, it does not amount to grace. There is nothing of Christ in morality; and that fruit is sour which grows not on the root Christ.

Moral actions are done out of a vainglorious humour, not any respect to God's glory. The apostle calls the heathen magistrates unjust (1 Corinthians 6:1). While they were doing justice in their civil courts, they were unjust; their virtues became vices, because faith was wanting, and they did all to raise them as trophies for their own praise and fame. So that morality is but the wild olive

of nature, it does not amount to grace. Heat water to the highest
degree, you cannot make wine of it, it is water still: so, let
morality be raised to the highest, it is nature still - it is but old
Adam put in a better dress. I may say to a civil man, 'yet lackest
thou one thing' (Mark 10:21). Moral virtue may stand with a
hatred of godliness. A moral man does as much hate holiness, as
he does vice. The Stoics were moralists and had sublime notions
about virtue, yet were the deadliest enemies St Paul had (Acts
17:18). So this is a counterfeit jewel.

(b) *Religious education is not the new creature.* Education
does much cultivate and refine nature; education is a good wall
to plant the vine of grace against, but it is not grace. King Jehoash
was good as long as his uncle Jehoiada lived; but when Jehoiada
died, all Jehoash's religion was buried in his uncle's grave (2
Kings 12:2). Have not we seen many who have been trained up
religiously under their parents, and were very hopeful, yet these
fair blossoms of hope have been blown off, and they have lived
to be a shame to their friends?

(c) *A form of godliness is not the new creature.* Every bird that
has fine feathers, has not sweet flesh; all that shine with the
golden feathers of profession, are not saints, 'Having a form of
godliness, but denying the power' (2 Timothy 3:5). What is a
lifeless form? Formality is the ape of piety; formalists may
perform all the external parts of religion - pray, fast, give alms.
Whatever duties a believer does in sincerity, the same may a
formalist do in hypocrisy. How devout were the Pharisees! How
humble was Ahab! What a reformer was Jehu! Yet this was but
a formal show of religion. Daedalus, by art, made images to move
of themselves, insomuch that people thought they were living;
formalists do so counterfeit, and play a devotion, that others think
they are living saints; they are religious charlatans.

(d) *Every change of opinion does not amount to the new
creature*; man may change from error to truth, yet be no new
creature. Here is a change in the head, but not in the heart; one may
be orthodox in his judgment, yet not cordially embrace the gospel;

he may be no papist, yet no true believer. He who is changed only in opinion, is but almost a Christian, and shall be but almost saved.

(e) *Every sudden passion, or stirring of the affections, is not the new creature*. There may be affections of sorrow; some, upon the reading the history of Christ's passion, may be ready to weep, but it is only a natural tenderness, which relents at any tragical sight. Affections of desire may be stirred, 'Lord, evermore give us this bread' (John 6:34): but these basely deserted Christ and would walk no more with him (verse 66). Many desire heaven but will not come up to the price. Affections of joy may be stirred. In the parable, the second sort of hearers are said to 'receive the word with joy' (Matthew 13:20). What was this but to have the affections moved with delight in hearing! Yet, that this did not amount to the new creature, is plain: firstly, because those hearers are said to have no root; secondly, because they fell away (verse 21). King Herod did hear John the Baptist gladly; he was much affected with John's preaching; where then was the defect? Why was not Herod a new creature? The reason was, because Herod was not reformed by the Baptist's preaching; his affections were moved, but his sin was not removed. Many have sweet motions of heart, and seem to be much affected with the word, but their love to sin is stronger than their love to the word; therefore all their good affections prove abortive, and come to nothing.

(f) *One may have trouble for sin, yet not be a new creature*. Trouble of spirit may appear, while God's judgments lie upon men; when these are removed, their trouble ceases, 'When he slew them, then they sought him; nevertheless they did flatter him with their mouths' (Psalm 78:34,36). Metal that melts in a furnace, taken out of the furnace returns to its former hardness: many in time of sickness seem to be like melted metal. What weeping and wringing of hands! What confessions of sin will they make! Do not these look like new creatures? But as soon as they recover, they are as bad as ever; their pangs go off again, and it never comes to a new birth.

(g) *A man may have the Spirit, yet not be a new creature*. The apostle supposes a case, that one might be made partaker of the Holy Ghost, yet fall away (Hebrews 6:4). A man may have some slight transient work of the Spirit, but it does not go to the root; he may have the common gifts of the Spirit but not the special grace; he may have the Spirit to convince him, not to convert him. The light he has is like a winter-sun, which has little or no influence - it does not make him more holy. He has the motions of the Spirit, but walks after the flesh.

(h) *Every abstaining from sin is not the new creature.* This abstaining may be firstly, from restraining grace, not renewing grace: as God withheld Laban from hurting Jacob (Genesis 31:24). The Lord may restrain men from sin, by the terror of a natural conscience. Conscience stands as the angel with a drawn sword, and saith, 'Do not this evil.' Men may be frighted from sin, but not divorced.

Secondly, men may abstain from sin for a while, and then return to it again; as Saul left off pursuing David for some time, and then hunted him again. This is like a man that holds his breath under water, and then takes breath again. 'Ye were now turned, and had done right in my sight: But ye turned and polluted my holy name' (Jeremiah 34:15,16).

Thirdly, men may leave gross sin, and yet live in more spiritual sins - leave drunkenness and live in pride, leave unclean-ness and live in malice. The Pharisee boasted he was no adulterer, but he could not say he was not proud or superstitious; here he left gross sin, and lived in spiritual sins.

Fourthly, men may leave sin partially - abstain from some sins, not all - they feed some sin in a corner. Herod left many sins, but one sin he lived in, that is, incest. All this does not amount to the new creature.

2. I shall show you wherein the essence of the new creature consists.
First, *in general.*
To the constituting of the new creature there must be a great

change wrought. He who is a new creature, is not the same man he was. He is of another spirit, 'My servant Caleb, because he had another spirit' (Numbers 14:24). When the harlot, Lais, came to one of her old acquaintance after he was converted, and tempted him to sin, *Ego non sum ego*, saith he, 'I am not the same man.' When one becomes a new creature, there is such a visible change that all may see it; therefore it is called a change 'from darkness to light' (Acts 26:18).

Paul, a persecutor, when converted, was so altered that all who saw him, wondered at him and could scarce believe that he was the same (Acts 9:21): as if another soul had lived in the same body.

Mary Magdalene, an unchaste sinner, when once savingly wrought upon, what a penitent creature did she become! Her eyes, that were enticements to lust, she takes penance of them, and washed Christ's feet with her tears; her hair, which she was so proud of, and which was a net to entangle her lovers, she now takes penance of it, and wipes Christ's feet with it.

Thus the new creature makes a visible change. Such as are the same as they were, as vain and proud as ever, here is no new creature to be seen: for then a mighty change would appear, 'And such were some of you, but ye are washed, but ye are sanctified ...' (1 Corinthians 6:11).

But every change does not evidence the new creature. First, there is a change from one extreme to another - from a prodigal to an usurer - from a Turk to a Papist. This is as if one should recover of one disease, and die of another.

Second, there is an outward change, which is like the washing of a swine. Ahab was much changed to outward view, when he 'rent his clothes, and put on sackcloth' (1 Kings 21:27), insomuch that God stands and wonders at him: 'Seest thou how Ahab humbleth himself?' Yet, for all this, he was but an hypocrite.

What change then is that which is requisite in the new creature?

It is an inward change, a change of heart. Though the heart be not new-made, it is new-moulded, 'Wash thy heart, O Jerusalem' (Jeremiah 4:14). Ahab's clothes were rent, but not his heart. The outward change will do no good without the inward. What will become of them then, who have not so much as an outward change? Thus you see in general, that, in the production of the new creature, there must be a change.

Secondly, *more particularly*
The change in the new creature consists in two things, and they are both set down in the text: 'old things are passed away; behold all things are become new.'

1. *'Old things are passed away.'*
Old pride, old ignorance, old malice; the old house may be pulled down ere you can set up a new.

But if all old things must pass away, then there are no new creatures. Who can be quite freed from sin? Does not Paul complain of a body of death?

We must know that the change wrought in the new creature, though it be a thorough change, yet it is not a perfect change; sin will remain. As there is a principle of grace, so of corruption; like wine and water mixed, there is, in the regenerate, flesh as well as spirit. Here a question arises.

If sin in the regenerate is not quite done away, then how far must one put off the old man, that he may be a new creature?

There must be a *grieving* for the remains of corruption, 'O wretched man that I am, who shall deliver me from this body of death?' (Romans 7:24). Paul did not cry out of his sufferings, his being beaten with rods, shipwrecked, stoned - but, like the bird of paradise - he bemoaned himself for sin. In the new creature there must be *quotidianus mugitus* - a daily mourning for the indwelling presence of corruption; a child of God does not wear sin as a gold chain, but as a fetter.

In the new creature there must be a *detestation* of old things, as one would detest a garment in which is the plague. It is not enough to be angry with sin; but we must hate it, 'I hate and abhor lying' (Psalm 119:163). Hatred is the highest degree of enmity; and we must hate sin not only for its hurtful effect, but for its loathsome nature; as one hates a toad for its poisonous quality.

In the new creature there is an *opposition* against all old things; a Christian not only complains of sin, but fights against it (Galatians 5:17).

But may not a natural man oppose sin?

Yes; but there is a great difference between his opposing sin, and the new creature's opposing it.

Firstly, there is a difference in the *manner* of opposition. The natural man opposes sin, only for the shame of it, as it eclipses his credit: but the new creature opposes sin for the filth of it - it is the spirit of mischief - it is like rust to gold, or as a stain to beauty. In addition, the natural man does not oppose all sin.

(a) He does not oppose inward sins; he fights against such sins as are against the light of a natural conscience, but not against heart-sins - the first risings of vain thoughts - the stirrings of anger and concupiscence - the venom and impurity of his nature.

(b) He does not oppose gospel sins - pride, unbelief, hardness of heart, spiritual barrenness; he is not troubled, that he can love God no more.

(c) He opposes not complexion-sins, such as the bias of his heart carries him more strongly to, as lust or avarice; he saith of his constitution-sins, as Naaman, 'In this thing, the Lord pardon thy servant' (2 Kings 5:18). But the new creature opposes all kinds of sin: as he that hates a serpent hates all kinds of serpents, 'I hate every false way' (Psalm 119:104).

Secondly, there is difference between the natural man's opposing sin, and the new creature's opposing sin, in regard of the *motives*. A natural man opposes sin, from carnal motives - to stop the mouth of conscience and to prevent hell. But the new creature opposes sin upon more noble motives - out of love to

God and fear of dishonouring the gospel.

In the new creature there is *mortifying* old corrupt lusts, 'They that are Christ's have crucified the flesh' (Galatians 5:24). The new creature is said to be 'dead indeed unto sin' (Romans 6:11). He is dead as to the love of sin, that it does not bewitch: and as to the power of it, that it does not command. The new creature is continually crucifying sin; some limb of the old Adam every day drops off. Though sin does not die perfectly, it dies daily. A gracious soul thinks he can never kill sin enough; he deals with sin as Joab with Absalom who took three darts in his hand and thrust them through the heart of Absalom (2 Samuel 18:14). So, with the three darts of faith, prayer, and repentance, a Christian thrusts through the body of sin; he never thinks this Absalom is enough dead.

Try then, if we have this first sign of the new creature, 'old things are passed away.' There is a grieving for sin, a detesting of it, an opposing to it, a mortifying of it; this is the passing away of old things, though not in a legal sense, yet in an evangelical; and though it be not to satisfaction, yet it is to acceptation.

2. *All things are become new*

The new creature is new all over; grace, though it be but in part, yet it is in every part. By nature every branch of the soul is defiled with sin, as every part of wormwood is bitter; so, in regeneration, every part of the soul is replenished with grace, therefore grace is called the 'new man' (Ephesians 4:24). Not a new eye, or a new tongue, but a new man - there are new dispositions, new principles, new aims - 'all things are become new.'

(a) In the new creature, there is *a new understanding*, 'Be ye renewed in the spirit of your mind' (Ephesians 4:23). The first thing an artist draws in a picture is the eye: when God newly draws us, and makes us new creatures, the first thing he draws in our souls is a new eye: the new creature is enlightened to see that which he never saw before.

He knows Christ after another manner. An unconverted man,

by the light of common grace, may believe Christ to be the Son of God: but the new creature knows Christ after another guise, manner, so as to esteem him above all, to adore him, to touch him by faith, to fetch an healing virtue from him.

The new creature knows himself better than he did. When the sun shines into a room, it discovers all the dust and cobwebs in it: so, when the light of the Spirit shines into the heart, it discovers that corruption which before lay hid; it shows a man his own vileness and nothingness, 'Behold, I am vile' (Job 40:4). A wicked man blinded with self-love, admires himself, like Narcissus that seeing his own shadow upon the water fell in love with it. Saving knowledge works self-abasement: 'Lord, thou art in heaven, and I am in hell,' said a martyr. Has this daystar of knowledge shined on our mind?

(b) The new creature is *renewed in his conscience*. The conscience of a natural man is either blind, or dumb, or seared; but conscience in the new creature is renewed. Let us examine, does conscience check for sin? The least hair makes the eye weep; and the least sin makes conscience smite. How did David's heart smite him for cutting off the lap of Saul's garment! A good conscience is a star to guide, a register to record, a judge to determine, a witness to accuse or excuse. If conscience does all these offices right, then it is a renewed conscience, and speaks peace.

(c) In the new creature *the will is renewed*. An old bowl may have a new bias put into it: the will, having a new bias of grace put into it, is strongly carried to good. The will of a natural man opposes God; when the wind goes one way and the tide another, then there is a storm: so it is when God's will goes one way and ours another. But when our will goes with God's, as the wind with the tide, then there is a sweet calm of peace in the soul - the sanctified will answers to God's will, as the echo to the voice, 'When thou saidst, Seek ye my face; my heart said unto thee, Thy face, Lord, will I seek' (Psalm 27:8). And the will being renewed, like the *primum mobile*, it carries all the affections along with it.

(d) The new creature has *a new conversation*. Grace alters a man's walk; before he walked proudly, now humbly; before loosely, now holily; he makes the Word his rule, and Christ's life his pattern, 'Our conversation is in heaven' (Philippians 3:20). As a ship that is sailing eastward, there comes a gale of wind and blows it westward: so, before a man did sail hellward, and on a sudden the Spirit of God comes upon him, and blows him heavenward; there is a new conversation. It was a speech of Oecolampadius, 'I would not speak nor do any thing that I thought Jesus Christ would not approve of, if he were here corporally present.' Where there is circumcision of heart, there is circumspection of life; if we find it thus, that 'all things are become new', then we are new creatures, and shall go to the new Jerusalem when we die.

Third use, Exhortation

Labour to be new creatures: nothing else will avail us, 'Neither circumcision availeth any thing, nor uncircumcision, but a new creature' (Galatians 6:15). We are for new things; we love new fashions, and why not new hearts? But people are full of prejudices against the new creature.

If we are new creatures, there must be so much strictness in religion, so much praying and watching, as discourages.

Is there any thing excellent to be obtained without labour? What pains is taken in searching for a vein of silver, or seeking for pearl? Men cannot have the world without labour; and would they have salvation so?

The labour in religion bears no proportion with the reward. What are a few tears shed, to a weight of glory? The soldier is content to wrestle with difficulties, and undergo a bloody fight, for a glorious victory. In all labour for heaven there is profit: it is like a man that digs in a golden mine, and carries away all the gold.

Men take more pains to go to hell; what pains does an

ambitious man take to climb to the pinnacle of honour? Tullia rode over the dead body of her father to be made queen. How does the covetous man tire himself, break his sleep, and his peace, to get the world? Thus some men take more pains in the service of sin, than others do in pursuit of holiness. Men talk of pains in religion; when God's Spirit comes into one it turns labour into delight. It was Paul's heaven to serve God (Romans 7:22). The ways of wisdom 'are ways of pleasantness' (Proverbs 3:17). It is like walking among beds of spices, which cast forth a sweet perfume.

But if we leave our old company, and become new creatures, we shall be exposed to many reproaches.

Who are they that speak evil of religion but such as are evil? *Male de me loquunter, sed mali*, said Seneca. Besides, is it not better that men reproach us for being good, than that God damn us for being wicked! 'Blessed are ye when men shall revile you' (Matthew 5:11). Stars are nevertheless glorious though they have ugly names given them, as the bear and the dragon. A saint's reproaches are like a soldier's scars, honourable, 'If ye are reproached for the name of Christ, the Spirit of God and of glory rests upon you' (1 Peter 4:14). While men clip your credit to make it weigh lighter, they make your crown heavier.

Having answered these objections, I come now to resume the exhortation: above all things labour to be new creatures.

Motives

Firstly, *in this true Christianity does consist*. It is not baptism makes a Christian: many are no better than baptized heathens. The essential part of religion lies in the new creature, 'Circumcision is that of the heart' (Romans 2:29). Every thing has a name from the better part. We call a man a reasonable creature, because of his soul, which is the more noble part: so one is called a Christian, because he acts from a principle of the new creature, which the carnal man does not.

Secondly, *it is the new creature which fits us for communion with God; we cannot converse with God till then.* Birds cannot converse with men unless they had a rational nature put into them, nor can men converse with God, unless, being made new creatures, they partake of the divine nature. Communion with God is a mystery to most; every one that hangs about the court does not speak with the king: all that meddle with holy duties, and, as it were, hang about the court of heaven, have not communion with God. It is only the new creature enjoys God's presence in ordinances, and sweetly converses with him as a child with a Father.

Thirdly, *the necessity of being new creatures.*

(1) *Till then we are odious to God,* 'My soul loathed them' (Zechariah 11:8). A sinner is to God worse than a toad; a toad has no poison, but what God has put into it: but a sinner has that which the devil has put into him, 'Why has Satan filled thy heart to lie?' (Acts 5:3). A wicked man is possessed with an evil spirit, one man is possessed with the devil of pride, another with the devil of malice - this must needs make persons odious to God, to be possessed with the devil. Thus it is till we become new creatures.

(2) *Till we are new creatures, our duties are not accepted with God*; they are but wild grapes.

(a) Because God accepts no man, but where he sees his image. The new creature is called the renewing of God's image (Ephesians 4:24). When they brought Tamarlane a pot of gold, he asked what stamp it had on it, and when he saw the Roman stamp on it, he refused it: so, if God does not see his own stamp and image on the soul, he rejects the most specious services.

(b) Duties of religion are not accepted without the new creature, because there is that wanting which should make them a sweet savour to God. The holy oil for the tabernacle was to be made of several spices and ingredients (Exodus 30:23): now if any of these spices had been left out, it had not been pleasing. The unregenerate man leaves out the chief spice in his duties, and that is faith: 'Without faith it is impossible to please God' (Hebrews

11:6). Faith lays hold on Christ and so is accepted.

(3) *Such as are not new creatures, but grow upon the stock of old Adam, get no benefit by ordinances*; they are to them, as dioscordium in a dead man's mouth; they lose their virtue. Nay, not only ordinances do them no good, but hurt. It were sad, if all a man did eat should turn to poison. The Word preached is a 'savour of death'; it is not healing, but hardening; nay, Christ himself is accidentally a 'rock of offence' (1 Peter 2:8). The wicked stumble at a Saviour, and suck death from the tree of life.

(4) *Without being new creatures, we cannot arrive at heaven*, 'There shall in no wise enter into it any thing that defileth' (Revelation 21:27). Heaven is not like Noah's ark, that received clean and unclean. A sinner is compared to swine (2 Peter 2:22), and shall a swinish creature tread upon the golden pavement of heaven? Indeed the frogs came into Pharaoh's court, but in heaven there is no entertainment for such vermin. It is only the new creature which qualifies us for glory: this consecrates the heart, and only the pure in heart shall see God. The new creature elevates the soul, as the loadstone elevates the iron. A soul renewed by grace, is fit to ascend to the heavenly glory.

Fourthly, *the excellency of the new creature.*

(1) The *nobility*. The new creature fetches its pedigree from heaven; it is born of God. God counts none else of the blood royal; it ennobles a man's spirit; he aspires after the favour of God, and looks no lower than a crown. The new creature raises one to honour; he excels the princes of the earth (Psalm 89:27), and is fellow-commoner with angels.

(2) The *immortality*. The new creature is begotten of the incorruptible seed of the Word, and never dies; it lasts as long as the soul, as angels, as heaven. God has laid out much cost upon it, and if it perish, he should lose all his cost. When Xerxes destroyed all the temples in Greece, he caused the temple of Diana to be preserved for its beautiful structure; the new creature is God's temple, adorned with all the graces, which he will not suffer to be demolished. Riches take wings, king's crowns tumble in the

dust; nay, some of the graces may cease: faith and hope shall be no more, but the new creature abideth for ever (1 John 2:27).

Fifthly, *the misery of the unregenerate creature*; dying so, I may say of him, as Christ said of Judas, 'Good were it for that man if he had never been born' (Mark 14:21). Better have been a toad, a serpent, any thing, if not a new creature; the old sinner must go into old Tophet (Isaiah 30:33). Damned caitiffs will have nothing to ease their torments - not one drop of honey in all their gall. In the sacrifice of jealousy there was no oil put to it (Numbers 5). In hell there is no oil of mercy put to the sufferings of the damned to lenify them.

Therefore get out of the wild olive of nature: labour to be new creatures, lest you curse yourselves at last. A sinful life will cause a despairing death.

What shall we do to be new creatures?

Wait on the ordinances. The preaching of the Word is the seed of which the new creature is formed; this is the trumpet which must make the dead in sin come out of their grave.

Pray earnestly for the new creature: 'Lord, thou hast made me once, make me again; what shall I do with this old heart? It defiles all it touches.' Urge God with his promise, 'A new heart also will I give you' (Ezekiel 36:26). Say, 'Lord, I am as the dry bones, but thou didst cause breath to come into them (Ezekiel 37:10). Do the same to me: breathe a supernatural life of grace into me.'

Use four, Thankfulness

Let such as are new creatures stand upon Mount Gerizim, blessing and praising God; ascribe all to the riches of God's love; set the crown upon the head of free grace. God has done more for you than if he had made you kings and queens; though you have not so much of the world as others, you are happier than the greatest monarchs upon earth; and, I dare say, you would not change with them. The apostles seldom speak of the new creation, but they join some thankful praises with it, 'Blessed be

God, who, according to his abundant mercy, hath begotten us again to a lively hope' (1 Peter 1:3); 'Giving thanks to the Father, who hath made us meet for the inheritance in light' (Colossians 1:12).

The new creature is a sign of election, a badge of adoption. What distinguishing love is this, that God should make any of us new creatures, when he hath left the greatest part of the world to perish in their sins! Such as are patterns of mercy, should be trumpets of praise.

3

The Evil Tongue

And the tongue is a fire, a world of iniquity
(James 3:6).

The apostle James in this Scripture, describes the evil of the tongue, 'The tongue is a fire, a world of iniquity.'

1. 'It is a fire.' It burns with intemperate heat; it causeth the heat of contention; it sets others in a flame.

2. 'A world of iniquity.' It was at first made to be an organ of God's praise, but it is become an instrument of unrighteousness. All the members of the body are sinful, as there is bitterness in every branch of wormwood, but the tongue is excessively sinful, 'full of deadly poison' (verse 8).

Doctrine: The tongue, though it be a little member, yet it hath a world of sin in it; the tongue is an unruly evil. I shall show you some of the evils of the tongue.

1. The evil tongue is the *silent* tongue; it is wholly mute in matters of religion; it never speaks of God or of heaven, as if it cleaved to the roof of the mouth. Men are fluent and discoursive enough in other things, but in matters of religion their lips are sealed up. If we come into some people's company, we do not know what religion they are of, whether Jews or Mohammedans, for they never speak of Christ; they are like the man in the gospel, who was possessed with a dumb spirit (Mark 9:17).

2. The evil tongue is the *earthly* tongue; men talk of nothing but the world, as if all their hopes were here, and they looked for an earthly eternity; these have earthly minds, 'He that is of the earth, speaketh of the earth' (John 3:31).

3. The evil tongue is the *hasty* or *angry* tongue; it has no

command of passions, but is carried away with them, as a chariot with wild horses. I know there is an holy anger, when we are angry with sin: Christ had this anger when they made the temple a place of merchandise (John 2:15). That anger is without sin, which is against sin; but that is an evil tongue, which is presently blown up into exorbitant passion; this 'tongue is set on fire from hell.' A wrathful spirit is unsuitable to the gospel; it is a gospel of peace, and its author is the Prince of Peace, and it is sealed by the Spirit, who came in the form of a dove, a meek peaceable creature. Thou who art given much to passion, whose tongue is often set on fire, take heed thou dost not one day in hell desire a drop of water to cool thy tongue.

4. The evil tongue is the *vain* tongue, that vents itself in idle words: 'Under his tongue is vanity' (Psalm 10:7). A vain tongue shows a light heart; a good man's words are weighty and prudent; his lips are as a tree of life to feed many and his speech is edifying, 'The tongue of the just is as choice silver' (Proverbs 10:20). But, 'The mouth of fools pours out foolishness' (Proverbs 15:2). How many idle away the day of grace in frivolous discourses? A wise man's words are like gold, weighty, and will sink into the hearts of others; but the words of many are light and feathery and will make no impression, 'Every idle word that men shall speak, they shall give an account thereof in the day of judgment' (Matthew 12:36).

5. The evil tongue is the *censorious* tongue, 'Who art thou that judgest another?' (James 4:12). Some make it a part of their religion to judge and censure others; they do not imitate their graces, but censure their failings. Such an one is an hypocrite, for this comes from pride. Were men's hearts more humble, their tongues would be more charitable. The censurer sits in the chair of pride, and passeth sentence upon another, and doth reprobate him; this is to usurp God's prerogative, and take his work out of his hands; it is God's work to judge, not ours. He who spends his time in censuring others spends but little time in examining himself and does not see his own faults. There is not a greater sign

of hypocrisy than to be overhasty in judging and censuring persons.

6. The evil tongue is the *slanderous* tongue, 'Thou sittest and slanderest thy own mother's son' (Psalm 50:20). Slandering is when we speak to the prejudice of another, and speak that which is not true. Worth and eminency are commonly blasted by slander; holiness itself is no shield from slander: 'John the Baptist came neither eating nor drinking, yet they say he hath a devil (Matthew 11:18). Come and let us smite him with the tongue. A slanderer wounds another's fame, and no physician can heal these wounds. The sword doth not make so deep a wound as the tongue. The Greek word for slanderer, signifies devil. Some think it is no great matter to belie and defame another; but know, this is to act the part of a devil. The slanderer's tongue is a two-edged sword, it wounds two at once; while the slanderer wounds another in his name, he wounds himself in his conscience. This is contrary to Scripture, 'Speak not evil one of another' (James 4:11). God takes this ill at our hands, to speak evil of others, especially such as are eminently holy, and help to bear up the honour of religion: 'Were ye not afraid to speak against my servant Moses?' (Numbers 12:8). What! My servant who hath wrought so many miracles - whom I have spoken with in the mount face to face - were not ye afraid to speak against him? So will God say, You must take heed of this, it is a sin your nature is very prone to; and remember, it is no less sin to rob another of his good name, than to steal his goods or wares out of his shop.

7. The evil tongue is the *unclean* tongue, that vents itself in filthy and scurrilous words, 'Let no corrupt communication proceed out of your mouth' (Ephesians 4:29). A sign of a great distemper, that the fever is high, is when the tongue is black: a sign men's hearts are very evil, when such black words come from them.

8. The evil tongue is the *lying* tongue, 'Lie not to one another' (Colossians 3:9). The Cretians were noted for liars (Titus 1:12). It becomes not Christians to be Cretians. Nothing is more

contrary to God than a lie; it shows much irreligion; lying is a sin that doth not go alone, it ushers in other sins. Absalom told his father a lie, that he was going to pay his vow at Hebron (2 Samuel 15:7), and this lie was a preface to his treason. Lying is such a sin, as takes away all society and converse with men; how can you have converse with him, that you cannot trust a word he saith? It is a sin so sordid, that when the liar is convicted, he is ashamed. God's children have this character, they are 'children that will not lie' (Isaiah 63:8), the new nature in them will not suffer them. The liar is near akin to the devil, and the devil will shortly claim kindred with him, 'The devil is a liar, and the father of it' (John 8:44). He seduced our first parents by a lie (Genesis 3:4). How doth this sin incense God? He struck Ananias dead for telling a lie (Acts 5:5). The furnace of hell is heated to throw liars into, 'Without are dogs, and sorcerers, and whosoever loveth and maketh a lie' (Revelation 22:15).

9. The evil tongue is the *flattering* tongue, that will speak fair to one's face, but will defame, 'He that hateth, dissembleth with his lips' (Proverbs 26:24). When he speaketh fair, believe him not; dissembled love is worse than hatred. Some can commend and reproach, flatter and hate - honey in their mouths, but a sting of malice in their hearts: better are the wounds of a friend, than the kisses of such an enemy. Hierom saith, 'The Arian faction pretended friendship; they (saith he) kissed my hands, but slandered me and sought my ruin.' Many have dissembling tongues, they can say, your servant, and lay snares, 'A man that flattereth his neighbour, spreadeth a net for his feet' (Proverbs 29:5). You oft think you have a friend in your bosom, but he proves a viper. To dissemble love is no better than to lie; for there is a pretence of that love which is not. Many are like Joab, 'And Joab said to Amasa, art thou in health, my brother? And he took him by the beard to kiss him, and he smote him in the fifth rib that he died' (2 Samuel 20:9). For my part, I must question his truth towards God, that will flatter and lie to his friend. God will bring such an one to shame at last, 'Whose hatred is covered by deceit, his wickedness shall be

shewed before the whole congregation' (Proverbs 26:26).

10. The evil tongue is the tongue given to *boasting*, 'The tongue is a little member, and boasteth great things' (James 3:5). There is an holy boasting, 'In God we boast all the day' (Psalm 44:8), when we triumph in his power and mercy: but it is a sinful boasting, when men display their trophies, boast of their own worth and eminency, that others may admire and cry them up; a man's self is his idol, and he loves to have this idol worshipped, 'There arose up Theudas, boasting himself to be somebody' (Acts 5:36). Sinful boasting is when men boast of their sins, 'Why boasteth thou thyself in mischief, O mighty man?' (Psalm 52:1). Some boast how wicked they have been; how many they have made drunk; how many they have deflowered; as if a beggar should boast of his sores; or a thief boast of being burnt in the hand. Such as boast of their sinful exploits, will have little cause to rejoice, or hang up their trophies when they come to hell.

11. The evil tongue is the *swearing* tongue, 'Swear not at all' (Matthew 5:34). The Scripture allows an oath for the ending of a controversy, and to clear the truth (Hebrews 6:16); but in ordinary discourse to use an oath, and so to take God's name in vain, is sinful. Swearing may be called 'the unfruitful works of darkness', there is neither pleasure nor profit in it; it is like an hook the fish comes to without a bait, 'Because of swearing the land mourneth' (Jeremiah 23:10). Some think it the grace of their speech; but, if God will reckon with men for idle words, what will he do for sinful oaths?

But it is only a petty oath, they swear by their faith?

Surely they which have so much faith in their mouth, have none in their heart. 'But it is my custom': Is this an excuse, or an aggravation of the sin? If a malefactor should be arraigned for robbing, and he should say to the judge, 'Spare me, it is my custom to rob on the highway'; the judge would say, 'Thou shalt the rather die.' For every oath thou swearest, God puts a drop of wrath into his vial.

But - may some think - what though now and then I swear an

oath? Words are but wind. But they are such a wind as will blow thee into hell, without repentance.

12. The *railing* tongue is an evil tongue: this is a plague-sore breaking out at the tongue, when we give opprobrious language. When the dispute was between the archangel and the devil about the body of Moses, 'The archangel durst not bring a railing accusation against him, but said, the Lord rebuke thee' (Jude 9). The archangel durst not rail against the devil. Railing oft ends in reviling, and so men bring themselves into a premunire, and are 'in danger of hell fire' (Matthew 5:22).

13. The *seducing* tongue is an evil tongue. The tongue that by fine rhetoric decoys men into error, 'By fair speeches deceive the hearts of the simple' (Romans 16:18). A fair tongue can put off bad wares; error is bad ware, which a seducing tongue can put off. The deceit lies in this; a smooth tongue can make error look so like truth, that you can hardly know them asunder; as thus, in justification, Christ bears infinite love to justified persons; this is a glorious truth, but under this notion, the Antinomian presseth libertinism; believers may take more liberty to sin, and God sees no sin in them. Thus, by crying up justification, they destroy sanctification; here is the seducing tongue; and error is as dangerous as vice; one may die by poison as well as by a pistol.

14. The evil tongue is the *cruel* tongue, that speaks to the wounding of the hearts of others. The tongue is made almost in the fashion of a sword; and the tongue is sharp as a sword, 'Their tongue is a sharp sword' (Psalm 57:4). Kind, loving words should be spoken to such as are of a heavy heart, 'To him that is afflicted pity should be shown' (Job 6:14). Healing words are fittest for a broken heart: but that is a cruel, unmerciful tongue, which speaks such words to the afflicted, as to cut them to the heart, 'They talk to the grief of those whom thou hast wounded' (Psalm 69:26). Hannah was a woman of a troubled spirit, 'She was in bitterness of soul, and wept sore' (1 Samuel 1:10). And now Eli, in verse 14, 'Said unto her, how long wilt thou be drunken? Put away thy wine from thee.' This word was like pouring vinegar into the

wound. When Job was afflicted with God's hand, his friends, instead of comforting him, told him he was an hypocrite (Job 11:2). These were cutting words, which went to his heart: instead of giving him cordials to his fainting, they use corrosives. This is to lay more weight upon a dying man.

15. The evil tongue is the *murmuring* tongue, 'These are murmurers' (Jude 16). Murmuring is discontent breaking out at the lips; men quarrel with God, and tax his providence as if he had not dealt well with them. Why should any murmur or be discontented at their condition? Doth God owe them anything? Or, can they deserve any thing at his hands? O, how uncomely is it to murmur at providence! It is fittest for a Cain to be wrath with God (Genesis 4:6).

(1) Murmuring proceeds from *unbelief.* When men distrust God's promise, then they murmur at his providence, 'They believed not his word, but murmured' (Psalm 106:24,25). When faith grows low, then passion grows high.

(2) Murmuring proceeds from *pride.* Men think they have deserved better; and, because they are crossed, therefore they utter discontented expressions against God. He who is humble bears any thing from God; he knows his punishment is less than his sin, therefore saith, 'I will bear the indignation of the LORD' (Micah 7:9). But pride raises discontent; and hence comes murmurings. Murmuring is a sin that God cannot bear, 'How long shall I bear with this evil congregation that murmur against me?' (Numbers 14:27). The murmurer discovers much ingratitude; a murmuring tongue is always an unthankful tongue; he considers not how much he is a debtor to free grace, and whatever he hath is more than God owes him; he considers not that his mercies outweigh his afflictions; there's more honey than wormwood in his cup; he considers not what God hath done for him, more than such as are better than he; he hath the finest of wheat, when others feed, as Daniel, on pulse. The murmurer, I say, doth not consider this; but, because he is crossed in some small matter, he repines against God. O ingratitude! Israel, though they had

manna from heaven, to satisfy their hunger, angel's food, yet murmured for want of quails; not content that God should supply their want, but must satisfy their lust too. O unthankful! Israel's murmuring cost many of them their lives, 'Neither murmur ye, as some of them did, and were destroyed of the destroyer' (1 Corinthians 10:10). Their speeches were venomous, and God punished them with venomous serpents.

16. The evil tongue is the *scoffing* tongue. The scoffer sits in the chair of scorners, and derides religion. Surely the devil hath taken great possession of men, when they have arrived at such a degree of sin, as to scoff at holiness. It was foretold as a sin of the last times, 'There shall come in the last days scoffers' (2 Peter 3:3). Some scoff at the authority of Scripture, the deity of Christ, the immortality of the soul; this is the worst sort of tongues. When men have laid aside the veil of modesty, and their consciences are seared, then they fall a scoffing at religion; and when once they are come to this, their case is desperate; no reproofs will reclaim them; tell them of their sin, and they will hate you the more, 'Reprove not a scorner, lest he hate thee' (Proverbs 9:8). Such a man is on the threshold of damnation.

17. The evil tongue is the tongue *given to cursing*, 'His mouth is full of cursing' (Psalm 10:7): a wishing some great evil to befall another; cursing is the scum that boils off from a wicked heart. Though it is true, the curse causeless shall not come - it is not in man's power to make another cursed - yet to wish a curse is a fearful sin. If to hate our brother be murder (1 John 3:15), then to curse him, which is the highest degree of hatred, must needs be murder. To use an execration or curse, is for a man to do what in him lies, to damn another. Some wish a curse upon themselves: so the Jews, 'his blood be upon us'. And so do your 'God damn-me's' as if damnation did not come fast enough: 'As he loved cursing so let it come to him' (Psalm 109:17).

18. The evil tongue is the *unjust* tongue; that will for a piece of money open its mouth in a bad cause. The lawyer hath *linguam venalem*, a tongue that will be sold for money, 'How long will

you judge unjustly?' (Psalm 82:2). Some will plead any cause, though never so bad: though it appears the deeds are forged, the witnesses bribed, there's perjury in the cause; yet they will plead it. When a man pleads a bad cause he is the devil's attorney: as God hates false weights, so a false cause. Better to be born dumb, than open one's mouth in a bad cause. O, what times are we in! Many pervert justice, and, for enriching themselves, overthrow a righteous cause; these are worse than they that rob, for they fleece men's estates under a colour of law, and ruin them under a pretence of doing justice.

Use 1.
Branch 1. See what a blow we have sustained by the fall; it hath put out of frame the whole course of nature. Original sin hath diffused itself as a poison into all the members of the body; it hath made the eye unchaste - the hands full of bribes - amongst the rest it hath defiled the tongue, 'it is a world of iniquity.' That which was made to be the organ of God's praise, is become a weapon of unrighteousness.

Branch 2. If there be so much evil in the tongue, what is the heart? If the stream be so full of water, how full of water is the fountain? If there be a world of iniquity in the tongue, how many worlds of sin are there in the heart, 'Their inward part is very wickedness' (Psalm 5:9). If the tongue, which is the outward part, be so wicked, the inward part is very wickedness, 'The heart is deep' (Psalm 64:6); it is such a deep as cannot be fathomed; deep pride, hypocrisy, atheism. The heart is like the sea, where is the leviathan, and creeping things innumerable (Psalm 104:25,26). If the skin hath boils of leprosy in it, how much corruption is in the blood? If the tongue be so bad, how diabolical is the heart? It is the heart sets the tongue a-work: 'Out of the abundance of the heart the mouth speaketh': there are the seeds of all atheism and blasphemy, 'Out of the heart proceed evil thoughts, murders, adulteries; these defile a man' (Matthew 15:19, 20). If a branch of wormwood be so bitter, then how bitter is the root? O, what a root of bitterness grows in a man's heart! Some say they have good hearts; but if the tongue be so bad, what is the heart? If I see a smoke come out of the top of a chimney, what a fire burns within? 'A wicked man walketh with a froward mouth; frowardness is in his heart' (Proverbs 6:12, 14). Solomon shows the reason why the mouth is so froward, 'Frowardness is in his heart.' The heart is a storehouse of wickedness, therefore called the 'evil treasure of the heart' (Matthew 12:35). Original righteousness was a good treasure, but we were robbed of that; and now there is an evil treasure of sin. The word treasure, denotes plenty; to show the fullness and abundance of sin that is in the heart. The heart is a lesser hell, which is a matter of deep humiliation; the heart is, like the Egyptian temples, full of spiders and serpents.

Use 2. Of reproof.

It reproves such as abuse their tongues in all manner of evil speaking, lying, slandering, rash anger. The heart is a vessel full of sin, and the tongue sets it abroach. O how fast do men's tongues gallop in sin! They say they give God their hearts, but they let the devil take possession of their tongues, 'Our lips are our own, who is the lord over us?' (Psalm 12:4). Who hath anything to do with our words? Who shall control us? Who is our lord? There is no engine the devil makes more use of than the tongue; what errors, contentions, impieties, have been propagated this way, to the dishonour of the High God! David calls his tongue his glory, 'Awake my glory' (Psalm 57:8). Why did he call his tongue his glory, but because by it he did set forth God's glory in praising him? But a wicked man's tongue is not his glory, but his shame; with his tongue he wounds the glory of God; 'it is set on fire of hell.'

Use 3. Confutation.

Branch 1. It confutes the Catharists and Perfectists, that plead for perfection in this life. If the tongue hath so many evils in it, how are they perfect? 'Who can say, I have made my heart clean, I am pure from sin?' (Proverbs 20:9). He makes a challenge to all the world. But the Perfectist saith, he is pure from sin: like Isidore the monk, *Non habeo Domine, quod mihi ignoscos*: I have nothing, Lord, for thee to pardon. If pure and perfect, then they put Christ out of office, he hath nothing to do for them as an advocate, they have no need of his intercession: but, 'There is not a just man upon earth, that doth good, and sinneth not' (Ecclesiastes 7:20). How proud and supercilious are they who hold they are perfect, when the holiest men alive, at some time or other, offend in their tongues? There is no perfection on this side the grave.

Branch 2. It confutes the Arminians, those patrons of free-will: they say, they have power to their own salvation - they can change their heart. The apostle saith, 'the tongue can no man tame' (James 3:8). If they cannot bridle their tongue, how can they master their will? If they cannot master this little member, how can they change their nature?

Use 4. Caution.

Take heed to your tongue; have a care that ye offend not with your tongue, 'Keep thy tongue from evil' (Psalm 34:14), 'I said, I will take heed to my ways, that I sin not with my tongue' (Psalm 39:1). An hard lesson! Pambas said he was above twenty years learning that Scripture, not to offend with his tongue. The tongue is an unruly member; God hath set a double hedge before the tongue, the teeth and the lips, to keep it within its bounds, that it should not speak vainly. O look to your tongue! When a city is besieged, he that keeps the gates of the city, keeps the whole city safe; so if you keep the gates or doors of your mouth, you keep your whole soul.

Rules for the well ordering and regulating your words, or the governing of your tongue, that you do not dishonour God therewith.

First rule. If you would have better tongues, labour for better hearts. It is the heart hath influence upon the tongue. If the heart be vain and earthly, the tongue will be so; if the heart be holy, the tongue will be so. Look to your heart, get a better heart, and a better tongue.

How shall I get my heart bettered?

Get a principle of grace infused. Grace is like the salt cast into the spring; grace changes the heart, and sanctifies all the members of the body - it sanctifies the eyes and makes them chaste - it sanctifies the tongue, and makes it meet and calm. When the Holy Ghost came upon the apostles, 'they began to speak with other tongues' (Acts 2:4): when God's Spirit comes on a man with a sanctifying work, he speaks with another tongue; the speech is heavenly. Grace makes the heart serious, and that cures the levity of the tongue; when the heart is serious, the words are savoury.

Second rule. If you would not sin in your tongue, call to mind how you have formerly offended in your tongue, and that will make you more watchful for the future. Have not you spoken words that have savoured of discontent or envy? Have not you been guilty of censuring and slandering? Have not you been disgusted with passion? Hath not your tongue out-run your discretion? Have not you spoken words that you have been sorry for afterwards, and have caused either shame or tears? O, observe former failings, how you have sinned in your tongue, and that will be a good help for the future! David certainly made a critical observation upon some of his words, wherein he had offended: words of pride, 'In my prosperity, I said, I shall never be moved' (Psalm 30:6). And 'I said in my haste all men are liars' (Psalm 116:11); even Samuel, and all the prophets who promised me the kingdom, they are all liars; and I shall die before I can come to enjoy it. David having observed how he had offended in his tongue, he is more careful of his words, and made a strict vow with himself, that he would look better to them, 'I said, I will take heed to my ways, that I sin not with my tongue' (Psalm 39:1). Look to the former slips of your tongue, and how you have by your words provoked God, and that will be a good means to make you more cautious for the future. A mariner that hath twice touched upon a rock, and been like to be cast away, will be more careful how he comes there again.

Third rule. Watch your tongue: most sin is committed for want of watchfulness. As the tongue hath a double fence set about it, so it had need have a double watch. The tongue, when it is let loose, will be ready to speak loosely; watch it, lest it run beyond its bounds in frothy and sinful discourse, 'If thou hast thought evil, lay thy hand upon thy mouth' (Proverbs 30:32): that is - say some - lay thy hand upon thy mouth, in token of repentance. But it may bear another sense: if thou hast thought evil, if angry malicious thoughts come into thy mind, lay thy hand upon thy mouth to stop thy lips, that thy thoughts come not into words.

Fourth rule. If you would not offend in your tongue, ponder your words well before you speak, 'Be not rash with thy mouth' (Ecclesiastes 5:2). Some speak vainly, because inconsiderately; they do not weigh their words before they speak them. A talkative man doth not mind his words, but gives his tongue liberty; he may speak not only inadvisably, but unholily, and give just offence.

Fifth rule. If you would not offend in your tongue, pray to God to guard your tongue, 'Set a watch, O LORD, before my mouth' (Psalm 141:3). Set not about this work in your own strength, but implore God's help; 'the tongue can no man tame' (James 3:8). But God can tame it; therefore go to him by prayer; pray, 'Lord, set a watch before the door of my lips'; keep me, that I may speak nothing to grieve thy Spirit, or that may tend to thy dishonour.

Sixth rule. If you would be kept from evil speaking, inure your tongue to good speaking. If you would not have the cask have a bad scent, put good liquor into it; so, if you would not have your tongue run out sinfully, let it be used to good discourse; speak often one to another of Christ, and the things pertaining to the kingdom of God. The spouse's lips dropped as an honeycomb (Canticles 4:11).

Motives to beware of tongue sins

First motive: If you have no care of your tongue, all your religion is vain, 'If any man among you seem to be religious, and bridleth not his tongue, this man's religion is vain' (James 1:26). Many an one will hear the word, and make a profession of religion, but cares not what liberty he takes in his tongue, to reproach and vilify others: this man's religion is vain; that is, (1) he hath no religion, his religion is but a show or pretence; (2) it is vain, because it is ineffectual; it hath not that force upon him as religion ought.

Second motive. The tongue discovers much of the heart; such as the tongue is, such commonly the heart is. A lascivious tongue shows a lustful heart; an earthly tongue a covetous heart; a murmuring tongue a discontented heart. The tongue is oft a commentary upon the heart.

Third motive. To allow ourselves in the abuse of the tongue, cannot stand with grace. I know a good man may sometimes speak inadvisably with his lips; he may fly out in words, be in a passion, but he doth not allow himself in it; when his passion is over, he weeps, 'that which I do, I allow not' (Romans 7:15). But, for a man to allow himself in sin, censuring, slandering, dropping words like coals of fire; surely it is not consistent with grace.

Fourth motive. The sins of the tongue are very defiling (James 3:6). They are defiling to one's self, and chiefly defiling to others. The tongue conveys poison into the ear of another; sometimes by false suggestions, raising prejudices in the mind of another against such a person; sometimes by passionate speeches, the spirit of another is provoked.

Fifth motive. The sins of the tongue are provoking to God, and prejudicial to us.

(1) Provoking to God (Psalm 106:33). Moses spake inadvisably with his lips; what was this unadvised speech? 'Hear now, ye rebels; must we fetch you water out of this rock?' (Numbers 20:10). Though he were a favourite, and God hath spoken with him face to face, yet God gives him a check for it; it turned his smile into a frown.

(2) Prejudicial to us; Moses' rash speech shut him out of Canaan; it may shut us out of heaven, of which that was but a type. Origen notes, Moses had sinned most in his tongue; and God punished him most in his tongue.

Sixth motive. He who offends not in his tongue, is a perfect man; an high expression; 'If any man offend not in word, the same is a perfect man' (James 3:2); that is, attains to a very high degree, in the highest form of Christ's school. A prudent man, or an upright man; or comparatively, in comparison of others, such as have not gotten the conquest over their passions, he is far above them, and, in comparison of them, he is a perfect man; such an one was holy Cranmer, that could not be provoked by the ill carriage of others, but requited injuries with kindness.

Seventh motive. You must give an account to God, as well of your speeches, as your actions, 'Every idle word that men shall speak, they shall give an account thereof in the day of judgment' (Matthew 12:36); words of no account, will have an heavy account. And, if God will reckon with men for every idle, angry word, then, what will he do for sinful oaths? 'Oh that my words were now written!' (Job 19:23). Truly, if many people's words were written, they would be ashamed of them. And, let me tell you, your words are written: 'The books were opened' (Revelation 20:12). In the book of God's remembrance all your words are written; you had need then be careful you offend not with your tongue; God writes down all you speak, and you must give an account to him. When Latimer heard the pen going behind the hangings, he was careful in his answers; and let me tell you, as your words are, such will your sentence be. When the books are opened, God will proceed with you in judicature, according to your words; by your words you shall be saved or condemned: 'By thy words thou shalt be justified, and by thy words thou shalt be condemned' (Matthew 12:37).

4

Not Being Weary in Well-doing

And let us not be weary in well-doing:
for in due season we shall reap, if we faint not
(Galatians 6:9).

In the verses before the text, the apostle had laid down a proposition, 'What a man soweth, that shall he reap' (verse 7); he that sows in sin shall reap in sorrow; he that sows the seeds of grace shall reap glory; there is the proposition. In the text, the apostle makes the application, let us not be weary in well-doing. We that have sown the good seed of repentance, and an holy life, 'Let us not be weary; for in due season we shall reap, if we faint not.'

1. An Exhortation: 'Let us not be weary.'
Where there is, (a) something implied - that we are apt to be weary in well-doing; (b) something expressed - that we ought not to be weary in well-doing.

(a) *The thing implied, that, we are apt to be weary in well-doing.* This weariness is not from the regenerate part, but the fleshly; as Peter's sinking in the water, was not from the faith in him, but the fear. This weariness in a Christian course is occasioned from four things:

(1) *From the revilings of the world*, 'My enemies speak against me' (Psalm 71:10). Innocency is no shield against reproach. But why should this make us weary of well-doing? Did not Jesus Christ undergo reproach for us, when the Jews put a crown of thorns on him, and bowed the knee in scorn? Is it any

dishonour to us to be reproached for doing that which is good? Is it any disparagement to a virgin to be reproached for her beauty and chastity? Our reproaches for Christ, we should bind as a crown about our head. Now a Spirit of glory rests upon us, 'If ye be reproached for the name of Christ, happy are ye; for the Spirit of God and of glory resteth upon you' (1 Peter 4:14). *Regium est bene facere et male audire.* He that clips our credit to make it weigh lighter, makes our crown heavier.

(2) That which is apt to occasion weariness in well-doing, is *the present sufferings we are exposed to*, 'We are troubled on every side' (2 Corinthians 4:8). But why should this make us weary in well-doing? Is not our life a warfare? It is no more strange to meet with sufferings in religion, than for a mariner to meet with storms, or a soldier to meet with bullets. Do not we consider upon what terms we are entered into religion? Did not we vow in baptism to fight under Christ's banner? Doth not our Lord tell us, we must take 'up the cross and follow' him? (Matthew 16:24). Is not this part of the legacy Christ hath bequeathed us? (John 16:33). We would partake of Christ's glory but not of his sufferings: besides, doth not many a man suffer for his sins? Do not men's lusts bring them to an untimely end? Do men suffer for their sins, and do we think much to suffer for Christ? How did St Paul rejoice in sufferings? (2 Corinthians 7:4). How did he glory in it? 'As a woman that is proud of her jewels,' said Chrysostom. Why should sufferings make us faint? Who would not be willing to tread upon a few thorns, that is going to a kingdom?

(3) That which is apt to occasion weariness in well-doing, is *the deferring of the reward*. We are apt to be discouraged and grow weary, if we have not what we desire presently; we are all for present pay. But consider first, our work is not yet done; we have not yet finished the faith; the servant doth not receive his pay till his work be done. Even Christ's reward was referred till he had done his work; when he had completed our redemption, and said upon the cross, 'It is finished,' then he entered into glory. Consider, secondly, that God defers the reward to make heaven

more welcome to us. After all our praying, weeping, suffering, how sweet will the joys of paradise taste!

(4) That which is apt to occasion weariness in well-doing, is *the greatness and difficulty of a Christian's work.* But why should this make us weary? Difficulty whets a generous mind; the soldier's life hath its difficulties, but they raise his spirits the more; he loves to encounter hardship, and will endure a bloody fight for a golden harvest. Besides, where is the least principle of grace, it renders the way of religion easy and pleasant. When the lodestone draws, it is easy for the iron to move. When God's Spirit draws we move in the way of religion with facility and delight. Christ's service is freedom. 'I will walk at liberty' (Psalm 119:45). To serve God, to love God, to enjoy God, is the sweetest liberty in the world. Besides, while we serve God, we gratify ourselves. As he who digs in a mine, while he sweats, he gets gold; while we glorify God, we promote our own glory.

(b) The second thing expressed is, that we should not grow weary in a Christian course - we should not tire in our race - 'Let us not be weary in well-doing.'

The Greek word, to be weary, signifies to shrink back, as cowards in war. Let it not be thus with us; let us not shrink back from Christ's colours, 'let us hold fast our profession' (Hebrews 4:14). We must not only hold forth our profession, but hold fast our profession. The crown is not given to him that fights, but to him that overcomes.

First Use. Of reproof

It reproves such as are weary of well-doing. These are falling stars. Demas forsook God (2 Timothy 4:10), and afterwards became a priest in an idol temple says Dorotheus. 'Israel hath cast off the thing that is good' (Hosea 8:3). Many have thrown off Christ's livery; they have left off an holy course of life; they have turned to worldliness or wantonness, 'Ye did run well, who did hinder you?' (Galatians 5:7). Why did you tire in your race? 'It had been better for them not to have known the way of righteousness, than, after they have known it, to turn from the holy commandment' (2 Peter 2:21).

Second Use. Exhortation: 'Let us not be weary in well-doing.' Consider,

(1) The way of religion is of good report (Hebrews 11:2). By faith 'the elders obtained a good report.' Shall we be weary of that which is our credit? If indeed the Christian religion were a thing that would bring shame or loss - as the ways of sin do - then we had cause to desert it, and grow weary of it. But it brings honour; 'She shall give to thy head an ornament of grace' (Proverbs 4:9). Why then should we be weary of well-doing?

(2) The beauty of a Christian is to hold on in piety without being weary: 'Mnason of Cyprus, an old disciple' (Acts 21:16). It is a beautiful sight to see silver hairs crowned with golden virtue. The beauty of a thing is when it comes to be finished; the beauty of a picture is, when it is drawn out in its full lineaments, and laid in its orient colours. The beauty of a Christian is when he hath finished his faith (2 Timothy 4:7). It was the glory of the church of Thyatira, she kept her best wine till last: 'I know thy works, and the last to be more than the first' (Revelation 2:19).

(3) Such as are weary of well-doing it is a sign they never acted in religion from choice, or from a principle of faith, but from the external spring of applause or preferment, so that, when these fail, their seeming goodness ceases.

(4) God is never weary of doing us good. Therefore we should not be weary of serving him. A king that is continually obliging his subjects by gifts and gratitudes, those subjects have no cause to be weary of serving their prince.

(5) If we grow weary, and throw off religion, we make all we have done null and void: 'When the righteous turneth away from his righteousness, all his righteousness that he hath done shall not be mentioned' (Ezekiel 18:24). He who hath been serving God, and doing angel's work, if once he grows weary and desists, he

unravels all his work, and misses of the recompense of reward. He that runs half a race, and then tires, loses the garland! O what folly is it to do well a while, and by apostasy to undo all! As if a limner with a pencil should draw a fair picture, and then come with his sponge and wipe it out again.

(6) Consider the examples of such as have continued their progress unweariably in a Christian course. The apostle sets before our eyes a cloud of witnesses; 'Being compassed about with so great a cloud of witnesses, let us run the race that is set before us' (Hebrews 12:1); let us run it with swiftness and constancy. How many noble martyrs and confessors of old, have walked in the ways of God, though they have been strewed with thorns? They scorned preferments, laughed at imprisonments, and their love to Christ burned hotter than the fire. Polycarp, when he came before the proconsul, and he bade him deny Christ, replied, 'I have served Christ these eighty-six years, and he hath not once hurt me, and shall I deny him now?' Tertullian saith, such was the constancy of the primitive saints, that the persecutors cried out, 'What a misery is this, that we are more weary in tormenting, than they are in enduring torment!' Let us tread in their steps, who through faith and patience inherit the promises.

(7) It will be our comfort on our deathbed, to review a well-spent life. It was Augustine's wish, that he might have a quiet, easy death. If anything make our pillow easy at death, it will be this, that we have been unweariable in God's work; this will be a deathbed cordial. Did you ever know any repent at death that they had been too holy? Many have repented that they have followed the world too much, not that they have prayed too much, that they have repented too much. What hath made death sweet, but that they have 'finished their course, and kept the faith.'

(8) Think of the great reward we shall have, if we do not give over, or grow weary, and that is, glory and immortality.

(a) This glory is ponderous; it is called a 'weight of glory' (2 Corinthians 4:17). The weight adds to the worth; the weightier a crown of gold is, the more it is worth.

(b) It is satisfying: 'I shall be satisfied, when I awake, with thy likeness' (Psalm 17:15). This glory will abundantly recompense all our labours and sufferings. The joy of harvest will make amends for all the labour in sowing. O what harvest shall the saints reap!

It will always be reaping time in heaven; and this reaping will be in due season; so the apostle saith in the text, 'We shall reap in due season.' The husbandman doth not desire to reap till the season. He will not reap his corn while it is green, but when it is ripe; so we shall reap the reward of glory in due season; when our work is done - when our sins are purged out - when our graces are come to their full growth - then is the season of reaping. Therefore let us not be weary of well-doing, but hold on in prayer, reading, and all the exercises of religion. We shall 'reap in due season, if we faint not.'

To keep us from fainting, know, that the reward promised is very near, 'Our salvation is nearer than when we believed' (Romans 13:11). We are but within a few days march of the heavenly Canaan; it is but a few more prayers and tears shed, and we shall be perfect in glory. As that martyr, Dr Taylor said, 'I have but one stile more to go over, and I shall be at my Father's house.' Stay but a while, Christians, and your trouble shall be over, and your coronation-day shall come. Christ who is the oracle of truth hath said, 'Surely I come quickly' (Revelation 22:20). And yet death's coming is sooner than Christ's personal coming, and then begins the saint's blessed jubilee.

What means shall we use, that we may not wax weary in a Christian course.

Let us shake off spiritual sloth which saith, 'There is a lion in the way.' He who is slothful, will soon grow weary; he is fitter to lie on his couch, than to run a race. It is a strange sight, to see a busy devil, and an idle Christian.

If we would not grow weary, let us pray for persevering grace. It was David's prayer, 'Hold thou me up, and I shall be safe' (Psalm 119:117). And it was Beza's prayer, 'Lord, perfect what thou hast begun in me.' That we may hold on a Christian course, let us labour for three persevering graces.

Faith keeps from fainting; faith gives a substance to things not seen, and makes them to be as it were present (Hebrews 11). As a perspective glass makes those things which are at a distance near to the eye, so doth faith: heaven, and glory seem near. A Christian will not be weary of service, that hath the crown in his eye.

The second persevering grace is *hope*. Hope animates the spirits: it is to the soul as cork to the net, which keeps it from sinking. Hope breeds patience, and patience breeds perseverance. Hope is compared to an anchor (Hebrews 6:19). The Christian never sins, but when he casts away his anchor.

The third persevering grace is *love*. Love makes a man that he is never weary. Love may be compared to the rod of myrtle in the traveller's hand, which refreshes him, and keeps him from being weary in his journey. He who loves the world is never weary of following the world; he who loves God will never be weary of serving him; that is the reason why the saints and angels in heaven are never weary of praising and worshipping God; because their love to God is perfect, and love turns service into delight. Get the love of God in your hearts, and you will run in his ways, and not be weary.

5

On Knowing God and Doing Good

To him that knoweth to do good,
and doth it not, to him it is sin
(James 4:17).

The apostle, in the former verses (13,14), had met with a sin common in those days, a sinful boasting among men, 'Go to now, ye that say, today or tomorrow, we will go into such a city, and buy and sell, and get gain; whereas you know not what shall be on the morrow' - you may be in your graves before tomorrow. 'For what is your life? It is even a vapour.'

A vapour being an exhalation, it cannot continue long; as it is raised by the sun so it is dispersed by the wind. Such is your life, a vapour, a short breath, a flying shadow, it appears for a 'little time, and then vanisheth.' Well might they say, what need we be taught such a plain lesson? Who knows not all this, that life is a vapour, and that we ought not to boast what we will do tomorrow? The apostle seems in the text to meet with them by way of answer, do ye know all this? Then the greater is your sin that you do it not, 'to him that knoweth to do good, and doth it not, to him it is sin.'

I shall only explain this phrase, 'to him it is sin'; that is, it is an heinous sin, it is sin with a witness. Every infirmity, everything that falls short of the rule is sin, much more, that which contradicts the rule. This man's sin hath an emphasis, it is a crimson sin, and it shall have a greater punishment; he that 'knew his lord's will, and did it not, shall be beaten with many stripes' (Luke 12:47). If he that sins ignorantly be damned, then he that sins knowingly shall be double damned.

1. That we ought to know to do good

We ought to be well-informed of those things which are to be done by us, in order to salvation. The Word written is a rule of knowledge, and the word preached is a commentary upon the word written; and both of them are to enrich our understanding, and to nurse us up in the knowledge of that which is good.

The reasons why we should know to do good, are:

1. Knowledge is our lamp and star to guide us in the truth. It shows us what we are to do, and what we are to leave undone. If we do not know that which is good, we can never practise it.

2. Knowledge is the foundation of all grace: of faith, 'They that know thy name, will put their trust in thee' (Psalm 9:10); and of love, 'This I pray, that your love may abound yet more and more, in knowledge' (Philippians 1:9); and of perseverance, the apostle joins these two, such as are unlearned, will be unstable.

3. The chief work in conversion consists in knowledge, 'Be ye transformed by the renewing of your mind' (Romans 12:2). The mind being renewed, the man is transformed. The first part of God's image consists in knowledge (Colossians 3:10).

4. There is nothing in religion, though never so excellent, can do us good without knowledge.

Use

See how necessary it is to get the knowledge of what is good; it ushers in salvation (1 Timothy 2:4). Ignorance of God is the cause of all sin (Jeremiah 9:3). Ignorance of God damns (Hosea 4:6). It is sad to be ignorant in gospel-times; but many alas! do not only not know God, but they are not willing to know, 'They refuse to know me, saith the LORD' (Jeremiah 9:6).

2. That we ought not only to know to do good, but to do it

This the apostle implies when he says 'to him that knows to do good, and doth it not'. The end of knowledge is practice. Search from one end of the Bible to the other, and you will find, that it is the practical part of religion is chiefly intended. The crown is not set upon the head of knowledge, but practice, 'Blessed are they that do his commandments, that they may have right to the tree of life' (Revelation 22:14).

Use 1

It shows us wherein most Christians are defective in the times of gospel. In the doing part of religion, they know how to do good, but do it not. They know they should abstain from evil and pursue holiness; but though they know this, yet they do it not.

(1) They know they should abstain from evil. Thus they know they should not swear (Matthew 5:34), yet they do it. They are more free of their oaths than their alms. They know uncleanness to be a sin; that it wastes the body, wounds the conscience, blots the name, and damns the soul (Galatians 5:19), yet they will go on in that sin, and for a cup of pleasure, drink a sea of wrath.

They know drunkenness to be a sin; that it doth make them like beasts, takes away their reason, unfits them for happiness, for they cannot think on going reeling to heaven; they know that God is preparing a cup for the drunkard (Revelation 16:19), yet for all that, they will not leave their drunken fits.

Men know that rash censuring is a sin, 'Speak not evil one of another, brethren' (James 4:11); yet they are guilty of this; they will not swear, but they will slander, and speak to the prejudice of others. They can never make them recompense for this; for no physician can heal the wounds of the tongue.

Thus they know that covetousness is a sin, yea, the root of all evil; yet the world engrosses all their time and thoughts; they thirst after gold more than grace, and labour more to have a full purse than a good conscience.

They know they should not vent their passions, 'If any man among you seem to be religious, and bridleth not his tongue, this man's religion is vain' (James 1:26). Origen observes of the rich man in the gospel, he had no water to cool his tongue, he had sinned most in his tongue, therefore was punished most in it. How unworthy is it for men to have their eyes and hands lifted up to heaven, and their tongues set on fire from hell; at one time praying, and another time cursing? How can such pray in a family, that are possessed with an angry devil? Thus men know they should abstain from evil, but they do it not.

(2) They know they should pursue holiness, but they do it not. They know they should read the Word, sanctify the Sabbath, use holy conference, pray in their families, redeem the time, walk circumspectly; they know to do good, but do it not.

Whence is it that men know to do good, yet do it not?

It is for *want of sound conviction*. Men are not thoroughly convinced of the necessity of practical godliness. They think there is a necessity of knowledge, because else there is no salvation; they will get some notions of Christ, that he is a Saviour, and has satisfied divine justice, and they hope they believe in him. Well then, we tell them that faith and obedience go together: that God is merciful, and though they are not so good as they should be, yet free grace will save them. Thus men content themselves with general notions of religion, but are not convinced of the practical part of godliness.

Men know to do good, yet do it not, because they are *not awakened out of their spiritual sloth*. It is easy to get the knowledge of a truth, to give assent to it, to commend it, to profess it; but to digest knowledge into practice, is the difficulty.

Men know to do good, but do it not, *through incredulity*; they are in part atheists. Did they believe that sin was so bitter, that wrath and hell followed it, would they not leave off their sins? Did they believe that to do the will of God was a privilege, religion was their interest, that there is joy in the way of godliness, and heaven at the end, would they not espouse holiness? But people, though they have some slight transient thoughts of these things, yet they are not brought to the belief of them. Therefore though they know to do good, yet they do it not. The reason why there are so few doers of the Word is because there are so few believers.

Men know to do good, but do it not, because *the knowledge*

in their head never works into their hearts. It doth not quicken them, nor warm their affections with love to the truth.

Men know to do good, but do it not, because of *prejudicate opinion*. The things to be done in religion are judged to be too strict and severe; they restrain sin too much, or they press too much to holiness.

Men know to do good, yet do it not, because they love their sin more than they love the Word: 'They set their heart on their iniquity' (Hosea 4:8). Some content themselves with having means of knowledge, 'Then said Micah, Now know I that the LORD will do me good, seeing I have a Levite to my priest' (Judges 17:13). But what is one the better to know what physic he should take, if he doth not take it.

Use 2. Of exhortation

Let me beseech all who have been hearers of the word, and have gotten a great measure of knowledge, that, as you know to do good, you would do it. This is the soul of religion. Luther says, I had rather do the will of God, than be able to work miracles.

Firstly, to do what you know, evidences your relation to Christ. You count it an honour to be near allied to the crown, but it is more honour to be akin to Christ.

Secondly, to know to do good, and do it, sets a crown upon the gospel, 'Your obedience is come abroad unto all men' (Romans 16:19); not your knowledge, but your obedience. To know to do good, and not to do it, hardens others in sin, scandalizes religion, and makes people ready to turn atheists. When some of the Spaniards came to Hispaniola, the Spaniards' carriage being loose and profane, the Indians asked them, What God they served? They answered, The God of heaven. The Indians replied, Sure your God is not a good God that hath such bad servants. Thus to know to do good, yet do it not, puts a scar in the face of religion, and brings an evil report upon it; but to do what we know, trumpets forth the fame of the gospel, and makes them that oppose it, to admire it.

Thirdly, to know to do good and to do it, entitles you to blessedness, 'He shall be blessed in his deed' (James 1:25): not for the deed, but in the deed.

3. That he who knoweth to do good, and doth it not, is of all others the most guilty.

To him it is crimson sin; that is, it is heinous sin, capital sin, sin emphatically, sin with a witness, and punished with a vengeance.

What is it to sin presumptuously?

To sin presumptuously, is to sin against the light which shines in a man's conscience, i.e. a man is convinced those things he doth are sin. Conscience saith, O do not this great evil! Conscience, like the cherubims, hath a flaming sword in its hand to affright, and deter the sinner; yet he will pluck the forbidden fruit. This is to sin presumptuously. This sin is highly aggravating, for three reasons:

(a) Because sinning presumptuously against conscience, is after counsels, admonitions, warnings. Such an one cannot say, he was never told of his sin; he hath had ministers rising up early, who hath told him what a damnable thing sin was, yet he would venture on; so that now he hath no excuse, 'Now you have no cloak for your sin' (John 15:22).

(b) It is an aggravation to sin presumptuously against conscience; when it is after afflictions. After God hath made him hear the voice of the rod, he hath made him to feel sin bitter, to read his sin in his punishment, yet he sins. His sin was following evil company, and God hath punished him for it; he hath almost wasted his estate with riotous living, or he hath almost drunk himself blind, yet he will not leave his sin; his sin was uncleanness, and his body is diseased, and full of noxious humours; yet though he feels the smart of sin, he retains the love of sin. Here is an aggravation of sin: 'In the time of his distress, did he trespass yet more against the LORD; this is that king Ahaz' (2 Chronicles 28:22).

(c) To know what is good, yet not to do it, is to sin presumptuously, is full of obstinacy and pertinaciousness. It is so, because men can say nothing for their sins, can bring no reason, they make no defence for themselves, yet they are resolved to hold fast their iniquity, like those in Jeremiah 18:12, 'And they said, there is no hope: but we will walk after our own devices, and we will every one do the imagination of his evil heart.'

Take heed of presumptuous sin
If God hath been so terrible against sins of infirmity and passion, as we see in Moses and Uzziah: O how fierce will his anger be against the presumptuous sinner! Better never have known the ways of God, than to know and not to do them! Oh! as you love your souls, take heed of this.

1. Presumptuous sins are desperate sins, because they are committed with much premeditation and forethought. The presumptuous sinner doth not sin unawares, but he doth project and cast in his mind how to bring his sin about, as Joseph's brethren did in betraying him, as Judas did in betraying Christ, and as those Jews did that laid wait for Paul.

2. Presumptuous sins are desperate, because they are accompanied with pride. The sinner who knows the mind of God, yet will act contrary to it, says, like Pharaoh, 'Who is the Lord that I should obey him?'

3. Presumptuous sins are desperate, because they are accompanied with impudency. Such sinners are hardened, fearless, and without shame. Like Judas, they are hardened; though woes be pronounced against them, they will sin; they are without fear like the leviathan (Job 41:33), and they have sinned away shame; 'The unjust knoweth no shame' (Zephaniah 3:5), he hath a forehead of brass. Nay, some are so far from blushing, that they glory in their shame (Philippians 3:19).

4. To sin presumptuously, to know what is good, yet not to do it, is heinous, because it is ingratitude; it is an high abuse of God's kindness; and God cannot endure, of all things, to have his

kindness abused. God's kindness is seen in this that he hath acquainted the sinner with his mind and will, that he hath not only instructed him, but persuaded him, made mercy stoop and kneel to the sinner, he hath wooed him with his Spirit, that he would flee from sin, and pursue holiness; kindness is seen in this, that God hath spared the sinner so long, and not struck him dead in the act of sin; kindness in this, that though the sinner hath sinned against his conscience, yet now, if he will repent of sin, God will repent of his judgments, and mercy shall be held forth, 'Thou hast played the harlot with many lovers; yet return again to me, saith the LORD' (Jeremiah 3:1). But the sinner is of a base spirit; he is not melted with all this love; but his heart like clay hardens under the sun. Here is an apparent abuse of God's kindness; and God cannot endure to have his kindness abused. The vulture draws sickness from perfumes; so the sinner contracts wickedness from the mercy of God. Here is high ingratitude.

5. To sin presumptuously, to know what is good, yet not to do it, is a contempt done to God. He cares not whether God be pleased or not, he will have his sin. Therefore the presumptuous sinner is said to reproach God, 'The soul that doth ought presumptuously, the same reproacheth the LORD' (Numbers 15:30). He reproacheth the Lord, though not explicitly, yet interpretatively. By his presumptuous sin he makes as if God was either ignorant, and did not know his wickedness; or impotent, and was not able to punish him. How horrid is this! There is a kind of blasphemy against God in every presumptuous sin.

6. To sin presumptuously, to know what is good, yet not to do it, is a bold contest with God, a daring of God to punish. The man that sins against conscience presumptuously, and will not be reclaimed, doth in effect say, What care I for the commandment? It shall be no check upon me, but I will go on in sin, and let God do his worst. A godly man is said to fear the commandment (Proverbs 13:13). He dares not sin, because the law of God stands in his way: but the presumptuous sinner doth not value the commandment; he will sin in spite of God's law. O desperate

madness, to dare God to his face! 'Do we provoke the Lord to jealousy? Are we stronger than he?' (1 Corinthians 10:22). Good reason then that we should take heed of presumptuous sin, since it is so heinous and desperate! 'To him that knows to do good, yet doth it not, to him it is sin'; it is sin with a witness.

Let us examine if we are not guilty of sinning thus presumptuously, knowing to do good, yet not to do it.

(1) Is it not to sin presumptuously, when we live in the total neglect of duty? We know we ought to pray in our families, yet do it not. To live in the neglect of family duties, is not this to sin presumptuously?

(2) Is it not to sin presumptuously, when we will venture upon the same sins which we condemn in others (Romans 2:1)? Thou (Christian) condemns another for pride, and yet thou lives in that sin thyself. A father condemns his son for swearing, yet he himself swears: the master reproves his servant for being drunk, yet he himself will be drunk. Is not this to sin presumptuously, to live in those sins which we condemn in others?

(3) Do not they sin presumptuously against conscience, who will sin in spite of heaven? Though they see the judgments of God executed on others, yet will adventure on the same sins? 'And thou his son, O Belshazzar, hast not humbled thy heart, though thou knewest all this' (Daniel 5:22); that is, thou sawest the judgments I inflicted on thy father.

(4) Do not they sin presumptuously, they who know to do good, yet do it not, who labour to stifle the convictions of their conscience, and will not let conscience speak freely to them? This the Scripture calls, 'holding the truth in unrighteousness' (Romans 1:18).

(5) Do not they sin presumptuously, who after they have felt the smart of sin, it hath bred a worm in their conscience, a moth in their estate; yet, after all this, they again embrace their sins.

That I may show you what you have to fear, and that I may beat you off from presumptuous sins, let these things be seriously laid to heart:

First, presumptuous sins do much harden the heart. These are two of the greatest blessings, a sound judgment and a soft heart; but sinning presumptuously and knowingly doth congeal the heart, it doth both waste the conscience and sear it (1 Timothy 4:2). By sinning knowingly, a person gets a custom of sin; and the custom of sinning takes away the sense of sinning, 'Being past feeling' (Ephesians 4:19). Tell the presumptuous sinner there are treasures of wrath laid up for him, he fears not; his heart is like a piece of marble or adamant that will take no impression. When men know to do good, yet do it not, their hearts are hardened insensibly, and that is dangerous.

Second, such as sin presumptuously, or they who know to do good, yet do it not, are self-condemned (Titus 3:11). The sinner knows in his conscience he is guilty; that he hath sinned against warnings, education and conviction; and therefore his own heart does and must condemn him. And when God judges and condemns him, he will clear his judge (Psalm 51:4).

Third, presumptuous sins make deep wounds in the soul. They lead to despair, and despair is the agony of the soul. Spira, in despair, was like a living man in hell; despair did suck out his marrow and vital blood making him a very anatomy. The sinner goes on stubbornly, yet his foolish heart tells him all will be well; but, when God begins to set his sins in order before him, and conscience, which was before like a lion asleep, begins to be awakened and roars upon him, and he sees death and hell before him, now his heart faints, his presumption is turned to despair, and he cries out as Cain, 'My punishment is greater than I can bear' (Genesis 4:13). Now the sinner begins to think with himself thus, I would have my sins and I had them; and now I have the wrath of God upon them. O how foolish was I to refuse instruction! But it is too late now; the mercy-seat is quite covered with clouds; I am shut out from all hopes of mercy; my wounds are such, that the balm of Gilead will not heal. The more presumptuous in the time of life, the more despair at the hour of death.

Fourth, to know to do good and not to do it, to sin presumptuously, God may, in just judgment, leave such an one to himself. It is a terrible thing, when God shall say, Thou hast, by thy presumptuous sin, affronted me, and provoked me to my face. Therefore, I will give thee up to thine own heart, thou shalt sin still; seeing thou wilt be filthy, thou shalt be filthy still.

Fifth, to know what is good, yet not to do it; to sin presumptuously, is a great degree of the sin against the Holy Ghost. Such as sin presumptuously, sin wilfully. Though presumption is not final apostasy, yet it comes very near to it; and a little matter more will make thee so guilty, that there remains no more sacrifice for sin. To sin presumptuously against light, may in time bring on malice and despite to the Spirit; as it was with Julian, who threw up his dagger in the air, as if he would be revenged on God. When once it is come to this, there is but one step lower a man can fall, and that is into hell.

Sixth, there is little hope for such as know to do good, yet do it not, know what is evil, but will not forbear. There were sacrifices for sins of ignorance, but no sacrifices for sins of presumption (Numbers 15:30). Indeed, presumptuous sinners hope all will be well, 'The fool rageth and is confident' (Proverbs 14:16). Such a fool is spoken of, 'When he heareth the words of this curse, he blesseth himself in his heart saying, I shall have peace, though I walk in the imagination of my heart, to add drunkenness to thirst: the LORD will not spare him, but the anger and jealousy of the LORD shall smoke against that man' (Deuteronomy 29:19,20).

Seventh, such as sin presumptuously, that know to do good, yet do it not, know what is evil, yet will not forbear it, God refuses all their services, whether reading, hearing, praying or communicating. God abhors their sacrifice, 'When you make many prayers, I will not hear you; your hands are full of blood' (Isaiah 1:15). And, 'They sacrifice flesh for the sacrifices of mine offerings; but the LORD accepted them not: now will he remember their iniquities, and visit their sins' (Hosea 8:13). Thus you see what cause you have to tremble, who are guilty in this kind: you see your misery.

Besides all that hath been said, consider these two things.

(1) You that sin presumptuously, that know to do good and do it not, that know what is evil, yet will not forbear, you cannot sin so cheaply as others; though sin will cost every one dear, yet it will cost you dearer. You go directly against conscience; and if there be either justice in heaven, or fire in hell, you shall be sure to be punished.

(2) You who sin presumptuously cannot take so much pleasure in your sin as another may have. One whose conscience is less enlightened, though his sin will be bitter to him afterwards, yet at present he may roll it as honey under his tongue, and find pleasure in it. But you that sin against your knowledge, you cannot have so much pleasure in sin as he, for conscience will put forth a sting, and all the threatenings of the Word will set themselves in battle array against you, so that you can have no quiet. And that trouble thou feelest now in thy conscience, is but the beginning of sorrow.

What shall we do, that we may not sin presumptuously against conscience?

Take heed of little sins; though, to speak properly, there are no such things as little sins, no little treason, but comparatively, one sin may be lesser than another. Take heed of little sins. The frequent committing of lesser sins will prepare for greater. A lesser distemper of the body, if it be let alone, prepares for a greater distemper, and being unjust in a little, prepares for being unjust in much (Luke 16:10). Such as were at first more modest, yet by accustoming themselves to lesser sins, by degrees their sins have grown up to a greater height; jail sins have begun at little sins.

If you would not sin presumptuously, that is, knowingly and wilfully, then reverence the dictates of conscience; and get conscience well-informed by the Word, as you set your watch by the sun, and then be ruled by it; do nothing against conscience. If conscience saith to do such a thing, though ever so unpleasing, set upon the duty. When conscience saith to take heed of such a thing, come not near the forbidden fruit. Conscience is God's deputy or proxy in the soul; the voice of conscience is the voice of God. Do not trifle with checks of conscience, lest God suffer thee to harden in sin, and by degrees come to presumptuous sin.

Labour to have your knowledge sanctified. Men sin against their knowledge, because their knowledge is not sanctified. Sanctified knowledge works upon the soul; inclining us to do good; making us flee from sin. Sanctified knowledge is like a breastplate which keeps the arrow of presumptuous sin from entering.

6

Christ All in All

But Christ is all in all
(Colossians 3:11).

The philosopher saith every science takes its dignity from the object; and the more noble the object, the more rare the knowledge. Hence it is, that Jesus Christ being the most sublime and glorious object, that knowledge which leads us to Christ must needs be most excellent; it is called 'the excellency of the knowledge of Christ' (Philippians 3:8). So sweet is this knowledge, that St Paul, 'determined to know nothing but Christ' (1 Corinthians 2:2). And indeed what needed he to know more? For 'Christ is all in all'. In the text there is a negation and an assumption: something the apostle sets down privatively, and something positively.

First, *privatively*
St. Paul tells the Colossians what will not avail them, 'neither circumcision, nor uncircumcision availeth'. Circumcision was a great privilege: a badge and cognizance to distinguish the people of God from those who were *exteri* and foreign; a pale between the garden enclosed, and the common. The people of circumcision were a people of God's circumspection, they were under his eye, and his wing, they were his household family; rather than that they should want, God would make the heavens a granary, and rain down manna upon them; he would set the rock abroach, and make it a lively spring. How glorious was circumcision! (Romans 9:4,5). What rich jewels hung upon Israel's crown! But

in matters of salvation, all this was nothing, 'neither circumcision nor uncircumcision'. From whence we may observe, that external privileges commend no man to God; whether wise, or rich, or noble, this doth not set us off in God's eye (1 Corinthians 1:26). God sees not as man sees. We are taken with beauty and parts, but these things avail not with God; God lays his left hand upon these, as Jacob did upon Manasseh (Genesis 48:14). God often passeth by those who cast a greater splendour and lustre in the world, and looks upon them of an inferior alloy. The reason is, 'that no flesh should glory in his presence' (1 Corinthians 1:29). If God should graft his grace only upon wisdom and parts, some would be ready to say, my wisdom, or my eloquence, or my nobility hath saved me; so therefore 'not many wise, not many noble are called.' God will have no priding or vaunting in the creature.

Use

Rest not in outward privileges or excellencies, for these are no stocks to graft the hopes of salvation upon, indeed many of Christ's kindred went to hell. Paul is called 'the servant of the Lord' (Romans 1:1). And James is called, 'the brother of the Lord' (Galatians 1:19). It is better to be the servant of the Lord, than the brother of the Lord. The virgin Mary was saved, not as she was the mother of Christ, but as she was the daughter of faith; it is grace, not blood gives the precedency. An heart that hath Christ formed in it is God's delight, and this brings me to the next.

Second, the apostle sets down something *positively*; but 'Christ is all in all'. In these words there is:

1. The subject, *Christ*. His name is sweet, it is 'as ointment poured forth' (Canticles 1:3). It was Job's wish, 'O that my words were now written! that they were graven with an iron pen and lead in the rock for ever!' (Job 19:23, 24). And it is my wish, O that this name, this sweet name, of Christ, were now written, that it were graven with the pen of the Holy Ghost in our hearts for ever.

The name of Christ hath in it, saith Chrysostom, a thousand treasuries of joy.

2. The predicate, 'all in all'. Christ is all fullness, all sweetness, he is all that is imaginable, all that is desirable. He who hath Christ can have no more, for 'Christ is all'.

The proposition out of the words is that Jesus Christ is the quintessence of all good things, 'he is all'.

Sometimes faith is said to be all (Galatians 5:6). Nothing availeth but faith; faith is all, as it is an instrument to lay hold on Christ, whereby we are saved; as a man is saved by catching hold on a bough.

Sometimes the new creature is said to be all (Galatians 6:15). Nothing availeth 'but a new creature'; the new creature is all, as it qualifies and fits for glory; 'without holiness no man shall see the Lord' (Hebrews 12:14). It is a saying of Chrysostom, at the day of judgment God will ask that question, as our Saviour did in Matthew 22:20, 'Whose is this image and superscription'. So will God say, Whose image is this? If thou canst not show him his image consisting in holiness, he will reject thee; thus the new creature is all.

Here in the text Christ is said to be all; but in what sense is Christ all?

Christ is all by way of eminency; all good things are eminently to be found in him, as the sun doth virtually contain in it the light of the lesser stars.

Christ is all, by way of derivation; all good things are transmitted and conveyed to us through Christ. As your rich commodities, jewels and spices come by sea, so all heavenly blessings sail to us through the red sea of Christ's blood: 'Through him and to him are all things' (Romans 11:36). Christ is that spiritual pipe, through which the golden oil of mercy empties itself into the soul. Christ must needs be all, for 'in him dwelleth all the fulness of the Godhead' (Colossians 2:9). He hath a partnership with God the Father: 'All things that the Father hath are mine' (John 16:15). So that there is enough in him to scatter all our fears, to remove all our burdens, to supply all our wants; there can be no defect in that which is infinite.

First Use: Information

It shows us the glorious fulness of Jesus Christ; 'he is all in all'. Christ is a panoply, a magazine and storehouse of all spiritual riches. You may go with the bee from flower to flower, and suck here and there a little sweetness, but you will never have enough till you come to Christ, for he is 'all in all'.

Christ is all in six respects:

(1) Christ is all in regard of righteousness. 'He is made to us righteousness' (1 Corinthians 1:30). The robe of innocency, like the veil of the temple, is rent asunder, for ours is a ragged righteousness: 'Our righteousness is as filthy rags' (Isaiah 64:6). As under rags the naked body is seen; so under the rags of our righteousness, the body of death is seen. We can defile our duties, but they cannot justify us; but Christ is all in regard of righteousness. 'Christ is the end of the law for righteousness to every one that believeth' (Romans 10:4); that is, through Christ we are as righteous as if we had satisfied the law in our own persons. Jacob got the blessing in the garment of his elder brother: so in the garment of Christ our elder brother, we obtain the blessing; Christ's righteousness is a coat woven without seam. 'We are made the righteousness of God in him.'

(2) Christ is all in regard of sanctification. 'He is made to us sanctification' (1 Corinthians 1:30). Sanctification is the spiritual enamel and embroidery of the soul. It is nothing else but God's putting upon us the jewels of holiness, and the angels glory by it, while we are made as the king's daughter, 'all glorious within' (Psalm 45:13). This doth tune and prepare the soul for heaven, turning iron into gold, making the heart which was Satan's picture, Christ's epistle. The virgins in Esther 2:12 had their 'days of purification'; they were first to be perfumed and anointed, and then they were to stand before the king. We must have the anointing of God (1 John 2:27), and be perfumed with

the graces of the Spirit, those sweet odours; and then we shall stand before the King of heaven. There must be first our days of purification before our days of glorification. What a blessed work is this! A soul beautified and adorned with grace, is like the firmament bespangled with glittering stars. O what a metamorphose is there! I may allude to that Canticle 3:6. So, who is this that comes out of the wilderness of sin, perfumed with all the graces of the Spirit? Holiness is the signature and engraving of God upon the soul. But whence is this? Christ is all; he is made to us sanctification; he it is that sends his Spirit into our hearts to be a refiner's fire, to burn up our dross, and make our graces sparkle like gold in the furnace. Christ ariseth upon the soul 'with healing in his wings' (Malachi 4:2). He heals the understanding, and saith, 'let there be light'; he heals the heart by dissolving the stone in his blood; and he heals the will, by filing off its rebellion. Thus he is all in regard of sanctification.

(3) Christ is all in regard of divine acceptance (Ephesians 1:6). He hath made us favourites, so Chrysostom and Theophylact render it; through Christ God is propitious to us, and takes all we do in good part. A wicked man being out of Christ, is out of favour; as his ploughing is sin (Proverbs 21:4), so his praying is sin (Proverbs 15:8). God will not come near him, his breath is infectious; God will hear his sins, and not his prayers. But now in Christ God accepts us (Ecclesiastes 9:7). As Joseph did present his brethren before Pharaoh, and brought them into favour with the king (Genesis 47:2), so the Lord Jesus carries the names of the saints upon his breast, and presents them before his Father, so bringing them into repute and honour; through Christ God will treat and parley with us, he speaks to us, as in Isaiah 62:4. Through the red glass every thing appears of a red colour; through the blood of Christ we look of a sanguine complexion, ruddy and beautiful in God's eyes.

(4) Christ is all in regard of divine assistance, for a Christian's strength lies in Christ (Philippians 4:13). Whence is it a Christian is able to do duty, to resist temptation, but through Christ's

strengthening? Whence is it that a sparkle of grace lives in a sea of corruption, the storms of persecution blowing, but that Christ holds this sparkle in the hollow of his hand? Whence is it that the roaring lion hath not devoured the saints, but that the Lion of the tribe of Judah hath defended them? Christ not only gives us our crown but our shield; he not only gives us our garland when we overcome, but our strength whereby we overcome: 'They overcome him, that is, the accuser of the brethren, by the blood of the Lamb' (Revelation 12:11). Christ keeps the fort-royal of grace that it be not blown up; Peter's shield was bruised, but Christ kept it that it was not broken. 'I have prayed for thee that thy faith fail not' (Luke 22:32), that it be not in a total eclipse. The crown of all the saints' victories must be set upon the head of Christ (Romans 8:38).

(5) Christ is all in regard of pacification. When conscience is in an agony, and burns as hell in the sense of God's wrath, then Christ is all and pours the balm of his blood into these wounds, and maketh the storm a calm. Christ doth not only make peace in the court of heaven, but in the court of conscience; he not only makes peace above us, but within us. Saith Cyprian, all our golden streams of peace flow from this fountain: 'Peace I leave with you, my peace I give unto you' (John 14:27). Jesus Christ not only purchased peace for us, but speaks peace to us; he is called the 'Prince of peace' (Isaiah 9:6). Thus Christ is all in regard of pacification. He makes peace for us, and in us; this honey and oil flow out of the rock Christ.

(6) Christ is all in regard of remuneration. He it is that crowns us after all our labours and sufferings. He died to advance us, and his lying in the wine-press was to bring us into the wine cellar; he is gone before, to take possession of heaven in the name of all believers: 'Whither the forerunner is for us entered, even Jesus' (Hebrews 6:20). Christ is gone to bespeak a place for the saints (John 14:2). He makes heaven ready for them, and makes them ready for heaven. Thus Christ is all in regard of remuneration: 'Behold, I come quickly, and my reward is with me' (Revelation 22:12).

Second Use

If Christ be all, it shows what a vast disproportion there is between Christ and the creature; there is as much difference as between *ens* and *nihil*; Christ is all in all, and the creature is nothing at all. 'Wilt thou set thine eyes on that which is not?' (Proverbs 23:5). The creature is a nonentity; though it hath a physical existence, yet considered theologically, it is nothing; 'tis but a gilded shadow, a pleasant fancy. When Solomon had sifted up the finest flour, and distilled the spirit of all created excellency, here is the result, 'All was vanity' (Ecclesiastes 2:11). We read the earth at its creation was void (Genesis 1:2): so are all earthly comforts void of that which we think is in them, and they are void of satisfaction, therefore they are compared to wind (Hosea 12:1). A man can no more fill his heart with the world, than he can fill his belly with the air he draws in. Now the creature is said to be nothing, in a threefold sense.

1. It is nothing to a man in trouble of spirit, for if the spirit be wounded, outward things will no more give ease than a crown of gold will cure a headache.

2. The creature is nothing to a man that hath heaven in his eye. When St. Paul had seen that light shining from heaven, surpassing the glory of the sun (Acts 26:13), though his eyes were open, 'he saw no man' (Acts 9:8). So he that hath the glory of heaven in his eye is blind to the world, he sees nothing in it to allure him or make him willing to stay here.

3. The creature is nothing to one that is dying. A man at the hour of death is most serious, and is able to give the truest verdict of things. Now at such a time the world is nothing, 'tis in an eclipse; the sorrow of it is real, but the joy imaginary. O then what a vast difference is there between Christ and the creature! Christ is 'all in all' and the creature nothing at all; yet how many damn their souls for nothing?

4. It shows whither the soul is to go in the want of all. Go to Christ who is all in all. Dost thou want grace? Go to Christ 'in whom are hid all the treasures of wisdom and knowledge'

(Colossians 2:3). Christ is the great Lord Treasurer. Go then to Christ and say, 'Lord, I am indigent of grace, but in thee are all my fresh springs, fill my cistern from thy spring. Lord, I am blind, thou hast eye-salve to anoint me; I am defiled, thou hast water to cleanse me; my heart is hard, thou hast blood to soften me; I am empty of grace, bring thy fulness to my emptiness.' In all our spiritual wants, we should repair to Christ, as Jacob's sons did to their brother Joseph: 'He opened all the storehouses' (Genesis 41:56), and 'gave to his brethren corn and provision for the way' (Genesis 42:25). Thus the Lord hath made Christ our Joseph. O then, sinners, make out to Christ; he is 'all in all'. And to encourage you to go to him, remember there is in him not only fulness, but freeness. 'O every one that thirsteth, come ye to the waters!' Christ is not only full as the honeycomb, but he drops as the honeycomb.

5. If Christ be all, see here the Christian's inventory, and how rich is he that hath Christ! He hath all that may make him completely happy. Plutarch reports that the wife of Phocion being asked where her jewels were answered, 'My husband, and his triumphs are my jewels!' So, if a Christian be asked where his riches are, he will reply, 'Christ is my riches.' A true saint cannot be poor, though if you look into his house, perhaps he hath scarce a bed to lie on: 'Even to this present hour, we both hunger and thirst, and are naked, and have no certain dwelling-place' (1 Corinthians 4:11). Come to many a child of God, and bid him make his will, he saith as Peter in Acts 3:6, 'Silver and gold have I none'. Yet he can at the same time make his triumph with the apostle in 2 Corinthians 6:10, 'As having nothing, yet possessing all'; he hath Christ who is all. When a believer can call nothing his, he can say all is his. The tabernacle was covered with badgers' skins (Exodus 25:5), yet most of it was gold; so a saint may have a poor covering, ragged clothes, but he is inlaid with gold for 'Christ is formed in his heart,' and so he is all glorious within.

6. But how can a Christian sit down satisfied with Christ!

'Christ is all.' What though he wants other things, is not Christ enough? If a man hath sunshine, he doth not complain he wants the light of a candle. Hath he not enough who hath the unsearchable riches of Christ? I have read of a godly man, who being blind, his friend asked him if he was not troubled for the want of his sight; he confessed that he was. 'Why,' saith his friend, 'are you troubled because you want that which flies have when you have that which angels have?' So I say to a Christian, Why art thou troubled for wanting that which a reprobate has, when thou hast that which the glorified saints have? Thou hast Christ with all his perquisites and royalties! Suppose a father should deny his son furniture for his house, but should settle all his land upon him, had he any cause to complain?

If God denies thee a little furniture in the world, but in the mean time settles his land upon thee and gives thee the field wherein the pearl of price is hid, hast thou any cause to repine? A Christian that wants necessaries, yet having Christ, he hath the one thing needful: 'Ye are complete in him' (Colossians 2:10). What! Complete in Christ, and not content with Christ? Luther saith that the sea of God's mercy should swallow up our particular afflictions; and surely this sea of God's love in giving us Christ should drown all our complaints and grievances. Let the Christian take the harp and the viol, and bless God.

7. If Christ be all, see the deplorable condition of a Christless person; he is poor, he is worth nothing. The sadness of a man that wants Christ, will appear in the following particulars.

He hath *no justification.* What a glorious thing it is when a poor sinner is absolved from guilt, and is declared to be *rectus in curia*! But this privilege flows from Christ; all pardons are sealed in his blood: 'By him all that believe are justified' (Acts 13:39). So he who is out of Christ is unjustified, for the guilt of sin cleaves to him. He must be responsible to justice in his own person, and the curse stands in full force against him.

He that wants Christ *wants the beauty of holiness,* for Jesus Christ is a living spring of grace, 'full of grace and truth' (John

1:14). Now a Christless person is a graceless person, and he hath not one shred of holiness. The scions must first be ingrafted into the stock, before it can receive sap and influence from the root; so we must first be ingrafted into Christ, before we can 'of his fulness receive grace for grace' (John 1:16). A man out of Christ is red with guilt, and black with filth; he is an unhallowed person, and dying in that condition, is rendered incapable of seeing God (Hebrews 12:14).

He that wants Christ hath *no true nobility*; for it is through Christ that we are akin to God, of the blood-royal of heaven; it is through Christ that 'God is not ashamed to be called our God' (Hebrews 11:16). But out of Christ we are looked upon as ignoble persons; the traitors' blood runs in our veins. A man out of Christ is base-born; whoever is his natural father, the devil is his spiritual father (John 8:44).

He that wants Christ *wants his freedom*: 'If the Son make you free, you shall be free indeed' (John 8:36). A man out of Christ is a slave, when he sins most freely.

He that wants Christ hath *no ability for service*. He is as Samson, when his locks were cut, his strength is gone from him. He wants a vital principle; he cannot walk with God; he is like a dead member in the body that hath neither strength nor motion: 'Without me ye can do nothing' (John 15:5). The organs will make no sound, unless you blow in them: so unless Christ by his Spirit breathe in the soul, it cannot make any harmony, or put forth strength to any holy action.

He that wants Christ *hath no consolation*; Christ is called the 'consolation of Israel' (Luke 2:25). A Christless soul is a comfortless soul; how can such an one have comfort when he comes to die? He is in debt, and hath no surety; his wounds bleed, and he hath no physician; he sees the fire of God's wrath approaching, and hath no screen to keep it off. He is like a ship in a tempest; sickness begins to make a tempest in his body, and sin to make a tempest in his conscience, and he hath nowhere to put in for harbour. Oh the terror and anguish of such a man at the hour of death! 'Their face shall be as flames' (Isaiah 13:8), an elegant expression. The meaning is, such fear and horror shall seize upon sinners in the evil day that their countenances shall change and be as pale as a flame. What are all the comforts of the world to a dying sinner? He looks upon his friends, but they cannot comfort him; bring his bags of gold and silver, they are as smoke to sore eyes, it grieves him to part with them; bring him music, what comfort is the harp and viol to a condemned man? There is in Spain tarantulas, venomous spiders, and those who are stung with them are almost dead, but are cured with music; but those that die without Christ, who is the consolation of Israel, are in such hellish pangs and agonies, that no music is able to cure them.

He that wants Christ *hath no salvation*: 'he is the Saviour of the body' (Ephesians 5:23). He saves none but those who are members of his body mystical, a strong Scripture against the doctrine of universal redemption. Christ leaped into the sea of his Father's wrath, only to save his spouse from drowning. 'He is the Saviour of the body', so that those who die out of Christ, are cut off from all hopes of salvation.

Third Use
It reproves them who busy themselves about other things with a neglect of Christ: 'Wherefore do you spend money for that which is not bread, and your labour for that which satisfieth not?' (Isaiah 55:2). If you get all the world, you are but golden beggars without Christ. The physician finds out noxious diseases, but is ignorant of soul-diseases; and while he gets receipts to cure others, he neglects the receipt of Christ's blood to cure himself. The lawyer, while he clears other men's titles to their land, he himself wants a title to Christ. The tradesman is busy in buying and selling, but neglects to trade for the pearl of price; like Israel, who went up and down to gather straw, or like the loadstone, that draws iron to it, but refuses gold. Those who mind the world, so as to neglect Christ, their work is but spider-work. 'Is it not of the LORD of

hosts that the people shall labour in the fire, and weary themselves for very vanity?' (Habakkuk 2:13).

If Christ be all, *then set a high valuation upon Jesus Christ*:
'To you which believe, he is precious' (1 Peter 2:7). If there were
a jewel which contained in it the worth of all jewels, would you
not prize that? Such a jewel is Christ; and so precious is he, that
Paul counted all things 'dung' that he 'might win Christ' (Philippians 3:8). O that I could raise the appreciation of Jesus Christ!
Prize Christ above your estates, above your relations; for that
man doth not deserve Christ at all who doth not prize Christ above
all. Jesus Christ is an incomprehensible blessing; whatever God
can require for satisfaction, or can desire for salvation, is to be
found in Christ. O then let him be the highest in our esteem! No
writing shall please me, saith Bernard, if I do not read the name
of Christ there. The name of Christ is the only music to a
Christian's ear, and the blood of Christ is the only cordial to a
Christian's heart.

If Jesus Christ be all, then *make sure of Christ*; never leave
trading in ordinances, till you have gotten this pearl of price. In
Christ there is the accumulation of all good things. O then let not
your souls be quiet, till this bundle of myrrh lie between your
breasts (Canticles 1:13)! In other things we strive for property,
saying this house is mine, these jewels are mine; and why is not
this Christ mine? There are only two words which will satisfy the
soul, deity and property. What was it better for the old world they
had an ark, as long as they did not get into the ark?

And that I may persuade all to get Christ, let me show you
what an enriching blessing Christ is.

(1) Christ is a supreme good. Put what you will in the balance
with Christ, he doth infinitely outweigh. Is life sweet? Christ is
better. He is the life of the soul (Colossians 3:4); 'his loving-
kindness, is better than life' (Psalm 63:3). Are relations sweet?
Christ is better. He is the friend that 'sticks closer than a brother.'

(2) Christ is a sufficient good. He who hath Christ needs no
more; just as he who hath the ocean needs not the cistern. If one

had a manuscript that contained all manner of learning in it, having all the arts and sciences, he need look in no other book; so he that hath Christ needs look no further. Christ gives grace and glory (Psalm 84:11). The one to cleanse us, the other to crown us; as Jacob said, 'It is enough, Joseph my son is yet alive' (Genesis 45:28). So he that hath Christ may say, It is enough, Jesus is yet alive.

(3) Christ is a suitable good. In him dwells all fulness (Colossians 1:19). He is whatever the soul can desire. Christ is beauty to adorn, gold to enrich, balm to heal, bread to strengthen, wine to comfort, salvation to crown. If we are in danger, Christ is a shield; and if we are disconsolate, he is a sun; for he hath enough in his wardrobe abundantly to furnish the soul.

(4) Christ is a sanctifying good. He makes every condition happy to us, he sweetens all our comforts, and sanctifies all our crosses.

Christ sweetens all our comforts for he turns them into blessings. Health is blessed, estate is blessed, relations are blessed. Christ's love is as the pouring sweet water on flowers, which makes them cast a more fragrant perfume. A wicked man cannot have that comfort in outward things which a godly man hath; for though he may possess more, he enjoys less. He who hath Christ may say, This mercy is reached to me by the hand of my Saviour, this is a love-token from him, an earnest of glory.

Christ sanctifies all our crosses, making them medicinal to the soul; they shall work sin out, and work grace in. God's stretching the strings of his viol is to tune it, and make the music better: Christ sees to it that his people lose nothing in the furnace but their drossy impurities.

(5) Christ is a rare blessing. There are but few that have him; the best things when they grow common, begin to be slighted; when silver was in 'Jerusalem as stones' (1 Kings 10:27), it was apt to be trod upon; Christ is a jewel that few are enriched with, which may both raise our esteem of him, and quicken our pursuit after him. Those to whom God hath given both the Indies, he hath

not given Christ; they have the fat of the earth, but not the dew of heaven. And there are among us Protestants, many who hear of Christ, but few that have him. Read Luke 4:25. There are many in this city who have Christ sounded in their ears, but few who have Christ formed in their hearts. O how should we labour to be of this few! They who are Christians should be restless.

(6) Christ is a select, choice good. God shows more love in giving us Christ, than in giving us crowns and kingdoms. God may give us other things, and hate us; but in giving Christ to a man, he gives him the blessings of the throne. What though others have a crutch to lean on? Abraham sent away the sons of the concubines with gifts, but 'he gave all he had to Isaac' (Genesis 25:5). God may send away others with a little gold and silver; but if he gives thee Christ, he gives thee all that ever he hath; for 'Christ is all, and in all.'

(7) Christ is such a good, as without which nothing is good. Without Christ health is not good, for it is fuel for lust; riches are not good, for they are golden snares. Ordinances are not good, though they are good in themselves, yet not good to us, for they profit not, being as breasts without milk, as bottles without wine, nay, they are not only a dead letter, but a savour of death. Without Christ, they will damn us; for want of Christ, millions go loaded to hell with ordinances.

(8) Christ is an enduring good. Other things are like the lamp, which while it shines it spends, and even the heavens 'shall wax old like a garment' (Psalm 102:26). But Jesus Christ is a permanent good, and with him are durable riches (Proverbs 8:18). They last as long as eternity itself lasts.

(9) Christ is a diffusive, communicative good; he is full, not only as a vessel, but as a spring, and he is willing to give himself to us.

Now then if there be all this excellency in Jesus Christ, it may make us ambitiously desirous of an interest in him.

But how shall I get a part in Christ?

See your need of Christ, and know that you are undone

without him. How obnoxious are you to God's eye! How odious to his nature! How obnoxious to his justice! O sinner, how near is the sergeant to arrest thee! The furnace of hell is heating for thee, and what wilt thou do without Christ? It is only the Lord Jesus can stand as a screen to keep off the fire of God's wrath from burning thee. Tell me then, is there not need of Christ?

Be importunate after Christ - 'Lord, give me Christ, or I die!' As Achsah said to her father Caleb in Joshua 15:19, 'Thou hast given me a south land, give me also springs of water', so should a poor soul say, 'Lord, thou hast given me an estate in the world, but this south land will not quench my thirst, give me also springs of water. Give me those living springs which run in my Saviour's blood, for thou hast said, 'Let him that is athirst come, and whosoever will let him take the water of life freely' (Revelation 22:17). Lord, I thirst after Jesus Christ, and nothing but Christ will satisfy me. I am dead, I am damned without him. O give me this water of life!'

Be content to have Christ, as Christ is offered, a Prince and a Saviour (Acts 5:31). Be sure you do not compound or indent with Christ. Some would have Christ and their sins too. Is Christ all, and will you not part with something for this all? Christ would have you part with nothing but what will damn you, namely, your sins. There are some bid fair for Christ, saying they will part with some sins, but keep a reserve. Doth that man think he shall have Christ's love that feeds sin in a corner? O part with all for him who is all! Part with thy lusts, nay thy life if Christ calls. It exhorts us not only to get Christ, but to labour to know that we have Christ: 'Hereby ye do know that we know him' (1 John 2:3). This reflex act of faith is more than the direct act. Some divines call it the perception, or sensible feeling, of faith.

Now concerning this knowledge that Christ is ours, which is the same with assurance, I shall lay down some corollaries or conclusions.

This knowledge is feasible

It may be had: 'These things have I written to you that believe, that ye may know ye have eternal life, and that ye may believe on the name of the Son of God' (1 John 5:13).

Why else doth God bid us make our 'calling and election sure' (2 Peter 1:10), if assurance may not be had, and to 'prove ourselves, whether we are in the faith' (2 Corinthians 13:5), if we cannot come to this knowledge that Christ is ours?

What are all the signs which the Scripture gives of a man in Christ but so many ciphers, if the knowledge of this interest may not be had? (1 John 3:14; 4:13).

There are some duties enjoined in Scripture which to perform is utterly impossible, if the knowledge of an interest in Christ be not attainable. We are bid 'to rejoice in the Lord' (Philippians 4:4) and 'to rejoice in tribulation' (1 Peter 4:13). How can he rejoice in suffering, who doth not know whether Christ be his or not?

Why hath Christ promised to send the Comforter (John 14:16), whose very work it is to bring the heart to this assurance, if assurance that Christ is ours may not be had?

Some of the saints have arrived at this certainty of knowledge; therefore it may be had. Job knew that his Redeemer lived (Job 19:25). And St. Paul had this assurance (2 Timothy 1:12, Galatians 2:20). But some may say that Paul being an eminent believer, a Christian of the first magnitude, no wonder if he had this jewel of assurance! Nay, but the apostle speaks of it as a case incident to other believers: 'Who shall separate us from the love of Christ?' (Romans 8:35). He doth not say, 'Who shall separate *me*?' but *us*! So a believer may come to spell out his interest.

Degrees of assurance

However, this is not to say that the saints have always the same certainty, or that they have such an assurance as excludes all doubtings and conflicts. There will be flowings and ebbings in their comforts, as well as in their graces. Was it not so with the

Psalmists? Sometimes we hear David say that God's loving-kindness was before his eyes (Psalm 26:3). As it is a proverbial speech, 'I have such a thing in my eye, I see it just before me.' But another, Ethan, wrote, 'Where are thy former loving-kindnesses?' (Psalm 89:49). These doubtings and convulsions God suffers in his children sometimes, that they may long the more for heaven, where they shall have a constant spring-tide of joy.

Nor do all believers have the same assurance. Assurance is rather the fruit of faith, than faith: now as the root of the rose or tulip may be alive, where the flower is not visible, so faith may live in the heart, where the flower of assurance doth not appear. However, assurance is difficult to be obtained; a rare jewel but hard to come by; and not many Christians have this jewel.

God sees it good sometimes to withdraw assurance from his people, that they may walk humbly. Satan doth what he can to waylay and obstruct our assurance; he is called 'the red dragon' (Revelation 12:3). If he cannot blot a Christian's evidence, yet sometimes he casts such a mist before his eyes, that he cannot read his evidence. The devil envies that God should have any glory, or the soul any comfort. But that we want assurance, the fault however for the most is our own; we walk carelessly, neglect our spiritual watch, let go our hold of the promises, and comply with temptations. No wonder then if we walk in darkness, and are at such a loss, that we cannot tell whether Christ be ours or not. Assurance is very sweet; this wine of paradise cheers the heart.

Assurance is very useful, for it will put us upon service for Christ
It will put us upon active obedience. Assurance will not, as the Papists say, breed security in the soul, but agility. It will make us mount up with wings as eagles, in holy duties; faith makes us living, assurance makes us lively. If we know that Christ is ours, we shall never think we can love him enough, or serve him enough: 'The love of Christ constrains us' (2 Corinthians 5:14).

Assurance will also put us upon passive obedience: 'We glory in tribulation ... because the love of God is shed abroad in our

hearts' (Romans 5:3, 5). Mr. Fox speaks of a woman in Queen
Mary's days, who when the adversaries threatened to take her
husband from her, she answered, 'Christ is my husband'; when
they threatened to take away her children, she answered, 'Christ
is better to me than ten sons'; when they threatened to take away
all from her, saith she, 'Christ is mine, and you cannot take away
him from me.' No wonder St. Paul was willing to be bound and
die for Christ (Acts 21:13); when he knew that Christ loved him,
and had given himself for him (Galatians 2:20). Though I will not
say that Paul was proud of his chain, yet he was glad of it, and he
wore it as a chain of pearl.

But how shall I get this jewel of assurance?
Make duty familiar to you. When the spouse sought Christ
diligently, she found him joyfully (Canticles 3:4).

Preserve the virginity of conscience. When the glass is full
you will not pour wine into it, but only when it is empty: so when
the soul is cleansed from the love of every sin, then God will pour
in the sweet wine of assurance: 'Let us draw near in full assurance
of faith, having our hearts sprinkled from an evil conscience'
(Hebrews 10:22).

Be much in the actings of faith. The more active the child is
in obedience, the sooner he hath his father's smile. If faith be
ready to die (Revelation 3:2), if it be like armour hung up, or like
a sleepy habit in the soul, never look for assurance.

If Christ be all, then make him so to you
(1) Make Christ all in your *understanding*, and be ambitious to
know nothing but Christ (1 Corinthians 2:2). What is it to have
knowledge in physic? To be able with Esculapius and Galen to
discourse of the causes and symptoms of a disease, and what is
proper to apply, and in the mean time to be ignorant of the healing
under Christ's wings? What is it to have knowledge in as-
tronomy, to discourse of the stars and planets, and to be ignorant
of Christ, that bright morning-star which leads to heaven? What

is it to have skill in a shop, and ignorant of that commodity which doth both enrich and crown? What is it to be versed in music, and to be ignorant of Christ, whose blood makes atonement in heaven, and music in the conscience? What is it to know all the stratagems of war, and to be ignorant of 'the Prince of peace'?

O make Christ all; be willing to know nothing but Christ. Though you may know other things in their due place, yet know Christ in the first place, and let the knowledge of Jesus Christ have the pre-eminence, as the sun among the lesser planets. This is the crowning knowledge: 'The prudent are crowned with knowledge' (Proverbs 14:18). We cannot know ourselves unless we know Christ, he it is who lights us into our hearts and shows us the spots of our souls, whereby we abhor ourselves in dust and ashes. Christ shows us our own vacuity and indigency, and until we see our own emptiness, we are not fit to be filled with the golden oil of mercy. We cannot know God, but through Christ (2 Corinthians 4:6).

(2) Make Christ all in your *affections*. Desire nothing but Christ; for he is the accumulation of all good things. 'Ye are complete in him' (Colossians 2:10). Christ is the Christian's perfection; and what should the soul desire less? What can it desire more? Love nothing but Christ; love is the choicest affection, it is the richest jewel the creature hath to bestow. O if Christ be all, love him better than all! If you love other things, when they die, your love is lost; but Christ lives for ever to requite your love. You may love other things in the excess, but you cannot love Christ in the excess. When you love other things, you love that which is inferior to yourselves; if you love a fair house, a pleasant garden, a curious picture, these things are inferior to yourselves. If I would love any thing more intensely and ardently, it should be something which is better than myself, and that is Jesus Christ. He who is all, let him have all: give him your love who desires it most, and deserves it best.

(3) Make Christ all in your *abilities*. Do all in his strength: 'Be strong in the Lord, and in the power of his might' (Ephesians

6:10). When you are to resist a temptation or to mortify a corruption, do not go out in your own strength, but in the strength of Christ. Some go out to duty in the strength of parts, and go out against sin in the strength of resolution, and they came home foiled. Alas! What are our resolutions, but like the green withs which did bind Samson! A sinful heart will soon break these. Do as David when he was to go up against Goliath; saith he, 'I come to thee in the name of the Lord.' So say to thy Goliath lust, I come to thee in the name of Christ. Then we conquer, when the Lion of the tribe of Judah marches before us.

(4) Make Christ all in your *aims*; do all to his glory (1 Peter 4:11).

(5) Make Christ all in your *affiance*; trust to none but Christ for salvation; the Papists make Christ something but not all. And is there not naturally a spice of popery in our hearts? We would be grafting happiness upon the stock of our own righteousness. 'Every man,' saith Luther, 'is born with a pope in his heart.' O make Christ all in regard of recumbency; let him be your city of refuge to flee to, and your ark.

(6) Make Christ all in your *joy* (Luke 1:47). 'God forbid that I should glory save in the cross of our Lord Jesus Christ' (Galatians 6:14). O Christian, hast thou seen the Lord Jesus? Hath this morning-star shined into thy heart with its enlightening, quickening beams? Then rejoice and be exceeding glad. Shall others rejoice in the world, and will not you rejoice in Christ? How much better is he than all other things? It reflects disparagement upon Christ when his saints are sad and drooping. Is not Christ yours, then what would you have more?

But, saith one, 'I am low in the world, and that takes off the chariot-wheels of my joy, and makes me drive heavily.'

But hast thou not Christ? And is Christ all? (Psalm 16:5,6).

If indeed I knew Christ were mine, then I could rejoice; but how shall I know that?

Is thy soul filled with pantings after Christ? Dost thou desire as well water out of Christ's side to cleanse thee, as blood out of his side to save thee? These sighs and groans are stirred up by the Spirit of God; by the beating of this pulse, judge of the life of faith in thee.

Hast thou given up thyself by an universal subjection to Christ? This is a good sign that Christ is thine.

Be thankful for Christ. God hath done more for you in giving you Christ, than if he had set you with the princes of the earth, (Psalm 113:8), or had made you angels, or had given you the whole world. In short, God cannot give a greater gift than Christ; for in giving Christ he gives himself to us; and all this calls aloud for thankfulness.

Comfort

Here is a breast of comfort to every man that hath Christ. It is good lying at this fountain-head. When a Christian sees a deficiency in himself, he may see an all-sufficiency in his Saviour. 'Happy is that people whose God is the LORD!' (Psalm 144:15). That servant needs not want who hath his master's full purse at command: he needs not want who hath Christ, for 'Christ is all and in all.' What though the fig-tree doth not flourish, if thou hast Christ the tree of life, and all fruit growing there? In the hour of death, a believer may rejoice; for when he leaves all, he is possessed of all. As Ambrose said to his friend, 'I fear not death, because I have a good Lord.' So may a godly man say, 'I fear not death, because I have a Christ to go to; death will but carry me to that torrent of divine pleasure which runs at his right hand for evermore.'

'Wherefore, comfort one another with these words' (1 Thessalonians 4:18).

7

The Preciousness of the Soul

For what is a man profited, if he shall gain the whole
world, and lose his own soul? or what shall a man give in
exchange for his soul? (Matthew 16:26).

Every man doth carry a treasure about with him, a divine soul;
and that this jewel should not be undervalued, he lays the soul in
balance with the whole world, and being put in the scales, the soul
weighs heaviest. 'What is a man profited, if he gain the whole
world, and lose his own soul?'

The world is a stately fabric, enriched with beauty and
excellency, like a curious piece of arras set about with divers
colours. It is a bright mirror and crystal, in which much of the
wisdom and majesty of God is resplendent. But as glorious as this
world is, every man doth carry a more glorious world about him,
a precious soul. It would bankrupt the world to give half the price
of a soul. It will undo the world to buy it, and it will undo him that
shall sell it. If we can save our souls, though we lose the world,
it is a gainful loss; if we lose our souls, though we gain the world,
our very gains will undo us. 'For what is a man profited, if he shall
gain the whole world, and lose his own soul? or what shall a man
give in exchange for his soul?'

The words branch themselves into these five parts:

1. A supposal of a purchase: 'if a man shall gain.' The
proposition is hypothetical; for Christ doth not say he shall gain,
but puts a case; it is not a certain purchase, it is only supposed.

2. The purchase itself: the world.

3. The extent of the purchase: the whole world, the world with
all its revenues and perquisites.

4. The terms of this purchase: 'he shall lose his soul', not that his soul shall be annihilated (that were happy), but he shall lose the end of his creation; he shall miss of glory, he shall lose his soul. And the loss of the soul is amplified by two things:

Firstly, the propriety, his own soul, that which is nearest to him, that which is most himself; the soul is the most noble part, it is the man of the man. He shall lose his own soul.

Secondly, the irrecoverableness of the loss: 'what shall a man give in exchange for his soul?' The words are a miosis, there is less said, and more intended. What shall he give? As if Christ had said, alas! he hath nothing to give; or, if he had something to give, yet nothing would be taken for it; for the soul cannot be exchanged, and there shall be no bail or mainprise taken for it. 'What shall a man give in exchange for his soul.'

5. Our Saviour's verdict upon this purchase: 'for what is a man profited?' as if Christ had said, he will have a hard bargain of it, he will repent him at last, it is but the fool's purchase: for what has he profited.

The observation is that the soul of man is a jewel more precious than a world; and all souls are of one price: in this sense that maxim in philosophy holds true, that all souls are alike. The souls of prince and peasant are all equal; and every soul of more value than a world. For the illustration of this doctrine there are two things to be demonstrated: first, that the soul is very precious; second, that it is more precious than a world.

1. The soul is very precious

What Job saith of wisdom, I may fitly apply to the soul: 'Man knows not the price thereof ... It cannot be valued with the gold of Ophir, with the precious onyx, or the sapphire. The gold and the crystal cannot equal it; and the exchange of it shall not be for jewels of fine gold' (Job 28:13, 16, 17). The soul is the glory of the creation; the soul is a beam of God; it is a sparkle of celestial brightness, as Demascen calls it; it is, according to Plato, a glass of the Trinity. There is in the soul an idea and resemblance of

God: an analogy of similitude, not proportion, as the schoolmen speak. If David did so admire the rare texture and workmanship of his body: 'I am wonderfully made, I was curiously wrought in the lowest parts of the earth' (Psalm 139:14, 15). If the cabinet be so curiously wrought, what is the jewel? How richly and gloriously is the soul embroidered! It is divinely inlaid and enamelled. The body is but the sheath: 'I was grieved in my spirit in the midst of my body' (Daniel 7:15); in the Chaldee it is, in the midst of my sheath. The most beautiful body is but like a velvet sheath, the soul is the blade of admirable metal. The soul is a sparkling diamond set in a ring of clay. The soul is a vessel of honour; God himself is served in this vessel. The soul is the bird of paradise that soars aloft; it may be compared to the wings of the cherubims, it hath a winged swiftness to fly to heaven. The soul is capable of communion with God and angels. The soul is God's house he hath made to dwell in. The understanding, will and affections are the three stories in this house. What pity is it that this goodly building should be let out, and the devil become tenant in it. The preciousness of the soul is seen in two particulars: first, it hath an intrinsical worth, and second an estimative worth.

The soul's intrinsical worth appears in two things: first, spirituality and second, immortality.

Spirituality
The soul is a spiritual substance. It is a saying among the ancients, that our souls are tempered in the same mortar with the heavenly spirits. Now the soul is spiritual in three manner of ways:

(1) The soul is spiritual in its *essence*. God breathed it in (Genesis 2:7). It is a sparkle lighted by the breath of God. The soul may be compared to the spirits of the wine, the body to the dregs: the spirits are the more pure refined part of the wine, such is the soul; the body is more feculent, while the soul is the more refined, sublimated part of man. Mistake me not, when I say the soul is spiritual, and that it is a beam of God; I do not mean that it is of the same substance with him, as Servetus, Osiander and others

have held; for when it is said God breathed into man the breath of life, they erroneously thought that the soul being infused did convey into man the spirit and substance of God, which opinion is absurd and sinful. If the soul should be part of the divine essence, then it will follow that the essence of God should be subject not only to change and passion, but which is worse, to sin, which would be blasphemy to assert. So when we say the soul is spiritual, the meaning is that God hath invested it with many noble endowments, and hath made it a mirror of beauty, and printed upon it a surpassing excellency; as the sun shining upon crystal, conveys its beauty, not its being.

(2) The soul is spiritual in its *object*, for it contemplates God and heaven; God is the orb and centre where the soul doth fix; if you could lift up a stone into the highest region, though it did break in a hundred pieces, it would fall to its centre. The soul moves to God, as to its rest: 'Return to thy rest, O my soul' (Psalm 116:7). He is the ark to which this dove flies; nothing but God can fill a heaven-born soul; if the earth were turned into a globe of gold, it could not fill the heart, it would still cry, Give, give. The soul being spiritual, God only can be the adequate object of it.

(3) The soul is spiritual in its *operation*, it being immaterial, it doth not depend upon the body in its working. The senses of seeing, hearing, and the rest of those organs of the body cease and die with the body, because they are parts of the body, and have their dependence on it; but the soul (as Aristotle saith) hath a nature distinct from the body, and it moves and operates of itself though the body be dead, and it hath no dependence upon, or coexistence with, the body. Thales Milesius, an ancient philosopher, calls the soul a self-moveable, for it hath an intrinsical principle of life and motion, though it be separate from the body. And thus you have seen the soul's spirituality.

Immortality

There are some that say the soul is mortal; indeed it were well for those who do not live like men, if they might die like beasts. But as Julius Scaliger well observes, it is impossible for any thing of a spiritual, uncompounded nature, to be subject to death and corruption: the souls of believers are with Christ after death (Philippians 1:23). Oecolampadias said to his friend who came to visit him on his deathbed, 'Good news, I shall be shortly with Christ my Lord.' And the devout soul shall be ever with the Lord (1 Thessalonians 4:17).

The heathens had some glimmerings of the soul's immortality. Cicero saith that the swan was dedicated to Apollo, because she sings sweetly before her death; by which hieroglyphic they intimated the joyousness of virtuous men before their death, as supposing the Elysian delights, which they should always enjoy after this life. And we read it was a custom among the Romans, that when their great men died, they caused an eagle to fly aloft in the air, signifying hereby that the soul was immortal, and did not die as the body.

The soul's immortality may be proved by this argument: That which is not capable of killing, is not capable of dying. The soul is not capable of killing; our Saviour Christ proves the minor proposition that it is not capable of killing: 'Fear not them that kill the body, and after that have no more that they can do' (Luke 12:4). Therefore the soul not being capable of killing, is not in a possibility of dying; the essence of the soul is metaphysical, having a beginning, but no end; it is eternal, a parly post. The soul doth not wax old, but lives for ever, which can be said of no sublunary created glory. Worldly things are as full of mutation as motion, and like Jonah's gourd, have a worm eating at the root.

The soul hath an estimative worth

Jesus Christ hath set a high value and estimate upon the soul; he made it, and he bought it, therefore he best knows the price of it. He did sell himself to buy the soul: 'They weighed for my price thirty pieces of silver' (Zechariah 11:12). Nay, he was content not only to be sold, but to die; this enhanceth the price of the soul, it cost the blood of God (Acts 20:28). Ye were not redeemed with corruptible things, as silver and gold, but with the precious blood of Christ (1 Peter 1:18). God must die, that the soul may live; the heir of heaven was mortgaged, and laid to pawn for the soul of man. What could Christ give more than himself? What in himself was dearer than his blood? O precious soul, that hast the image of God to beautify thee, and the blood of God to redeem thee! Christ was the priest, his divine nature the altar, his blood the sacrifice which he did offer up as an atonement for our souls. Now reckon what a drop of Christ's blood is worth, and then tell me what a soul is worth.

Satan doth value souls, he knows their worth; he saith as the king of Sodom did to Abraham, 'Give me the persons, and take the goods to thyself.' So saith Satan, 'Give me the persons.' He cares not how rich you are, he doth not strive to take away your estates, but your souls. Give me the persons, saith he, take you the goods; whence are all his *noemata*, his warlike stratagems, his subtle snares, but to catch souls? Why doth this lion so roar but for his prey? He envies the soul its happiness, he lays the whole train of tentation to blow up the whole fort-royal of the soul. Why doth he lay such suitable baits? He allures the ambitious man with a crown; the covetous man with a golden apple; the sanguine man with beauty. Why doth he tempt to Delilah's lap, but to keep you from Abraham's bosom? The devil is angling for the precious soul; to undo souls is his pride; he glories in the damnation of souls; it is next to victory to die revenged. If Samson must die, it is some comfort that he shall make more die with him; if Satan, that lion, must be kept in his hellish den, it is all the heaven he expects, to reach forth his paw, and pull others into the den with him.

2. The soul is more precious than a world

Having showed you the soul's preciousness; the next thing to be demonstrated is that the soul is more precious than a world. The world is made of a more impure lump; the world is of a coarser make, of an earthly extract; the soul is heaven-born, of a finer spinning, of a more noble descent; the world is a great book or volume, wherein we read the majesty and wisdom of him that made it; but the soul is the image of God (Genesis 1). The soul is a studied piece; for when God made the world, it was but *fiat*, let it be, and it was done; but when he made the soul, all the persons in the Trinity sat together at the council table: 'Come, let us make man in our own likeness' (Genesis 1:26). The soul is a glass wherein some rays of divine glory shine, and much of God is to be seen in it. Though this glass be cracked by the fall, yet it shall one day be perfect; we read of spirits of just men made perfect (Hebrews 12:23). The soul since the fall of Adam, may be compared to the moon in its conjunction, very much obscured by sin; but when it is sanctified by the Spirit, and translated from hence, it shall be as the moon in the full, shining forth in its perfect glory.

If the soul be so precious, see then what that worship is that God doth expect and accept; namely, that which comes from the more noble part of the soul.

In Psalm 25:1, David did not only lift up his voice, but his soul: 'To thee, O LORD, do I lift up my soul'. Though God will have the eye and the knee, the service of the body; yet he complains of them that draw near with their lips, when their hearts were far from him (Isaiah 29:13). The soul is the jewel; David not only put his lute and viol in tune, but his soul in tune to praise God: 'Bless the LORD, O my soul' (Psalm 103:1); his affections joining together in worship made up the concert. The soul is altar, fire and incense; it is the altar on which we offer up our prayers, the fire which kindles our prayers, and the incense which perfumes them. God's eye is chiefly upon the soul: bring an hundred dishes to table, he will carve of none but this; for this is the savoury meat he loves. He who is best will be served with the best; when we give him the soul in a duty, we give him the flower and the cream; by a holy chemistry we still out the spirits. A soul inflamed in service is 'the cup of spiced wine, and the juice of the pomegranate' (Canticles 8:2), which the spouse makes Christ to drink of. Without the worship of the soul, all our religion is but bodily exercise which profits nothing; without the soul we give God but a carcase. What are all the Papists' fastings, penance, pilgrimages, but going to hell in more pomp and state? What are the formalist's prayers, which do even cool between his lips, but a dead devotion? It is not sacrifice but sacrilege; for he robs God of that which he hath a right to, his soul.

If the soul be so precious, then of what precious account should ordinances and ministers be?

Ordinances are the golden ladder by which the soul climbs up to heaven; they are conduits of the water of life. O how precious should these be to us! They that are against ordinances, are against being saved.

Of how precious account should ministers be, whose very work is to save souls; their feet should be beautiful.

Their labours should be precious; they are, in the Greek, *sunergoi* (2 Corinthians 6:1). They labour with God, and they labour for your souls; all their sweat, their tears, their prayers are for you; they woo for your souls, and oftentimes spend their lives in the suit.

Their liberty should be precious. Constantine was a great honourer of the ministry; if indeed you see any of them who are of this holy and honourable function, like that drug the physicians speak of, which is hot in the mouth, but cold in operation; if you see them either idle or ravenous, if they do not divide the word rightly, and live uprightly, censure and spare not. God forbid I should open my mouth for such. In the law, the lips of the leper were to be covered; that minister who is by office an angel, but by his life a leper, ought to have his lips covered, he deserves silencing. A good preacher but a bad liver is like a physician that hath the plague; though his advice and receipts which he gives may be good, yet his plague infects the patient: so though ministers may have good words, and give good receipts in the pulpit, yet the plague of their lives infects their people. If you find a Hophni and Phinehas among the sons of Levi, whose unholy carriage makes the offering of God to be abhorred, you will save

God a labour in ejecting them. But be sure you distinguish between the precious and the vile; while you let out the bad blood, have a care to preserve the heart-blood; while you purge out the ill humours, do not destroy the spirits; while you are taking away the snuffs, do not eclipse the lights of God's sanctuary; it is a work fit for a Julian to suppress the orthodox ministry, and open the temple of the idol. The Romans sacked the city of Corinth, and raised it down to the ground for some incivility offered to their ambassador. God will avenge the affronts offered to his ministers (Psalm 105:15). O take heed of this! If souls be of such infinite value, how precious should their liberties be, whose very design and negotiation is to save souls (1 Timothy 4:16; Jude 23).

If the soul be so precious, take heed of abusing your souls. Socrates exhorted young men that they should look their faces in a glass, and if they saw they were fair, they should do nothing unworthy of their beauty. Christians, God hath given you souls that sparkle with divine beauty; O do nothing unworthy of these souls, do not abuse them.

There are four sorts of persons that abuse souls.

Firstly, they degrade their souls that set the world above their souls; 'Who pant after the dust of the earth' (Amos 2:7). As if a man's house were on fire, and he should take care to preserve the lumber, but let his child be burnt in the fire. Further, they degrade their souls that make their souls lackeys to their bodies. The body is but the brutish part, the soul is the angelical; the soul is the queen-regent, who is adorned with the jewels of knowledge, and sways the sceptre of liberty. Oh what a pity it is that this excellent soul shall be made a vassal, and be put to grind in the mill, when the body in the meantime sits in a chair of state! Solomon complains of an evil under the sun: 'I have seen servants upon horses, and princes walking as servants upon the earth' (Ecclesiastes 10:7). Is it not an evil under the sun to see the body riding in pomp and triumph, and the soul of man, that royal and heaven-born thing, as a lackey walking on foot.

Secondly, they abuse their souls that sell their souls.

The covetous person sells his soul for money. As it is said of the lawyer, he hath a tongue that will be sold for a fee, so the covetous man hath a soul that is to be set for money. Achan did sell his soul for a wedge of gold. Judas did sell his soul for silver; Judas sold cheap pennyworths; for thirty pieces of silver he did sell Christ, who was more worth than heaven; and his own soul which was more worth than a world! How many have damned their souls for money? (1 Timothy 6:9, 10). It is observed that the eagles' quills or feathers mixed with hens' feathers, will in time consume them. Such is the world to the soul; for if you mix these earthly things with your souls, and let them lie too near you, they will in time consume and undo your souls.

The ambitious person sells his soul for honour; as Alexander the Sixth did sell his soul to the devil for a popedom; and what is that honour but *res imaginaria*? A torch lighted by the breath of people, with the least puff of censure blown out! How many souls have been blown into hell with the wind of popular applause?

The voluptuous person sells his soul for pleasure. As Heliogabalus drowned himself in sweet water, so many drown their souls in the sweet perfumed waters of pleasure. Plato calls pleasure the bait that catcheth souls. Pleasure is a silken halter, a flattering devil, which kills with embracing.

Thirdly, they abuse their souls that poison their souls; for error is a sweet poison. Ignatius calls it the invention of the devil. A man may as well damn his soul by error as vice, and may as soon go to hell for a drunken opinion as for a drunken life.

Fourthly, they abuse their souls that starve their souls. These are they that say they are above ordinances; but surely we shall not be above ordinances, till we are above sin. The apostle saith, that in the blessed sacrament we are to remember the Lord's death till he come (1 Corinthians 11:26), that is, until Christ comes to judgment. How then can any omit sacraments without a contempt and affront offered to Christ himself? If Saint Paul and the apostles, those giants in grace, needed the Lord's Supper to confirm and corroborate them, how much more do we need such holy ordinances, who have but an infant faith. But Satan likes these fasting days, he would have men fast from ordinances: if the body be kept from food, it cannot live long.

If the soul be so precious a thing, take heed you do not lose your souls.

Consider what a loss it is, as appears in two things.

(1) It is a *foolish* loss to lose the soul, 'Thou fool, this night thy soul shall be required of thee' (Luke 12:20). It is a foolish loss to lose the soul, in a threefold respect.

(a) Because there is a possibility of saving the soul. We have time to work in, we have light to work by, we have the Spirit offering us help. The soul is like a ship laden with jewels, while the Spirit is a gale of wind to blow; and if we would but loosen anchor from sin, we might arrive at the port of happiness.

(b) It is a foolish loss, because we lose the soul for things of no value; worldly things are infinitely below the soul, they are nonentities. 'Wilt thou set thine eyes upon that which is not?' (Proverbs 23:5). The world is but a bewitchery, whose things glister in our eyes; but at death we shall say we have set our eyes on that which is not. He that thinks to find happiness here is like Ixion, that hugged the cloud instead of Juno, and like Apollo, that embraced the laurel-tree instead of Daphne. Now to lose the soul for such poor inconsiderate things is a foolish thing. It is as if one should throw a diamond at a pear-tree, and thereby he loseth his diamond.

(c) It is a foolish loss, for a man to lose his soul, because he himself hath a hand in it. Is it not folly to give one's self poison? A sinner hath his hands imbrued in the blood of his own soul: 'thy destruction is of thyself' (Hosea 13:9). 'They lay wait for their own blood' (Proverbs 1:18). The foolish sinner nourisheth those lusts that kill his soul. The tree breeds the worm, and the worm eats the tree. Were it not folly for a garrison to open to the enemy that besiegeth it; yet the sinner opens to those lusts which war against his soul (1 Peter 2:11), this is a foolish loss.

(2) It is a *fatal* loss to lose the soul.

(a) It is an unparalleled loss, because in losing the soul there are so many things lost with it; as a merchant in losing his ship loseth many things with it; his money, plate, jewels, spices. Thus he that loseth his soul, he loseth Christ, he loseth the Comforter, he loseth the society of angels, he loseth heaven.

(b) It is an irreparable loss. Other losses may be made up again; if a man lose his health, he may recover it again; if he lose his estate, he may get it up again; but if he lose his soul, this loss can never be made up again. Are there any more saviours to die for the soul? As Naomi said to her daughters, 'Are there yet any more sons in my womb?' (Ruth 1:11). Hath God any more sons? Or will he send his Son any more into the world? Oh no, if the soul be lost, Christ's next coming is not to save it, but to judge it! Christian, remember thou hast but one soul, and if that be gone, all is gone. God, saith Chrysostom, hath given thee two eyes, if thou losest one, thou hast another; but thou hast but one soul, and if that perish, thou art quite undone. The merchant that ventures all in one ship, if that ship be lost, he is quite broken.

(c) The loss of the soul is an eternal loss; for the soul once lost, is lost for ever; the sinner and the furnace shall never be parted (Isaiah 33:14). As the sinner's heart will never be emptied of sin, so God's vial shall never be emptied of wrath: it is an eternal loss.

Do what you can to secure the main chance, to save these precious souls.

In times of danger men call in their debts, and labour to secure their estates. Let me tell you, all you who are yet in your natural estate, your souls are mortgaged. If your land were mortgaged, you would endeavour to redeem it. Your souls are mortgaged: sin hath mortgaged them, and hath laid your souls to pawn, and where do you think your souls are? The pawn is in the devil's hand, therefore a man in the state of nature is said to be 'under the power of Satan'(Acts 26:18). Now there are but two ways to fetch home the pawn, and both are set down in Acts 20:21: 'Repentance towards God, and faith towards our Lord Jesus Christ.' Unravel all your works of sin by repentance, honour Christ's merits by believing: divines call it saving faith, because upon this wing the soul flies to the ark Christ, and is secured from danger.

8

The Soul's Malady and Cure

They that are whole need not a physician,
but they that are sick
(Luke 5:31).

The occasion of the words is set down in the context: Levi was called from the receipt of custom (he was a custom-house man), but Christ called him, and there went out power with the word, 'for he left all, rose up, and followed him' (verse 28). Levi did not consult with flesh and blood, he did not say, 'What shall I do for the hundred talents?' (2 Chronicles 25:9). How shall I live and maintain my charge? I shall lose many a sweet bit at the custom-house; poverty is like to be my patrimony; nay, in case I follow Christ, I must espouse persecution; he doth not reason thus; but having a call, he hastens away after Christ, 'he rose up and followed him'; and that he might give Christ a pledge and specimen of his love, he makes him a feast (verse 29). 'And Levi made him a great feast in his own house'; a better guest he could not invite. Christ always came with his cost; Levi feasted Christ with his cheer, and Christ feasted him with salvation.

Well, Christ being at this feast, the Pharisees begin to murmur, 'Why do ye eat and drink with publicans?' (verse 30). Firstly, the Pharisees were offended at him that he should go in and eat with publicans. The publicans were counted the worst of sinners; sinners of the deepest dye. Yet the Pharisees were not so much offended at the sins of the publicans, as they had a mind to pick a quarrel with Christ. He who was the horn of salvation to some, was a rock of offence to these Jews; others did feed on him, these did stumble at him. Secondly, they accuse Christ: for these words carry in them a charge and accusation, 'Why do ye eat with publicans and sinners?' The Pharisees impeached Christ for eating with sinners; malice will never want matter of accusation. Though the devils proclaimed Christ's holiness: 'Let us alone, I know thee who thou art, the Holy One of God' (Luke 4:34), yet the Pharisees tax him for being a sinner. See what malice will do, it will make a man speak that which the devil himself will not speak. The devils justify Christ, the Pharisees accuse him. And if Christ, who was a Lamb without spot, could not escape the world's censures, it is no wonder if his people are loaded with the calumnies and censures of the wicked.

But let us examine the matter of the charge they bring against Christ, and see how groundless it was. They indict Christ for going in with sinners.

Firstly, Christ did nothing but what was according to his commission; the commission he received from his Father, was, that he should come to save sinners (1 Timothy 1:15).

Secondly, Christ went in with sinners, not to join with them in their sins, but to heal them of their sins. To accuse Christ was, as Austin saith, as if the physician should be accused, because he goes among them that are sick of the plague. This groundless accusation Christ overhears, and in the text gives these envious Pharisees a silencing answer, 'They that are whole need not a physician, but they that are sick.' As if Christ had said, You Pharisees think yourselves righteous persons, you need no Saviour; but these poor publicans are sick and ready to die, and I come as a physician to cure them; therefore be not angry at a work of mercy; though you will not be healed, yet do not hinder me from healing others. 'They that are whole need not a physician, but they that are sick.'

In the words there are two general parts: firstly, the dying patients, and secondly, the healing physician.

1. The dying patients: them that are sick.
Sin is a soul-disease (Psalm 103:3); the Hebrew of Isaiah 53:4, 'He hath borne our *griefs*,' is our sicknesses.

Man at first was created in a healthful temper, he had no sickness of soul, he ailed nothing; the soul, in the Greek, had its *eukrasia*, its perfect beauty and glory. The eye was clear, the heart pure, the affections tuned with the finger of God into a most sweet harmony. God made man upright (Ecclesiastes 7:29); but Adam, by eating the apple, fell sick; and had died for ever, had not God found out a way for his recovery.

For the amplification of this doctrine, there are three things to be considered: (1) In what sense sin is resembled to sickness; (2) What the diseases of the soul are; (3) That sin-sickness is the worst.

In what sense sin is resembled to sickness
1. Sin may be compared to sickness for the manner of catching.
First, sickness is caught often through carelessness; some get cold by leaving off clothes. So when Adam grew careless of God's command, and left off the garment of his innocency, he caught a sickness; he could stay no longer in the garden, but lay bedrid; his sin hath turned the world which was a paradise into an hospital.

Secondly, sickness is caught sometimes through superfluity and intemperance. Excess produceth sickness. When our first parents lost the golden bridle of temperance, and did eat of the forbidden tree, they and all their posterity surfeited on it, and took a sickness. The tree of knowledge had sickness and death under the leaves; it was fair to the eye (Genesis 3:6), but poison to the taste. We all grew desperately sick by eating of this tree. Adam's intemperance hath brought us to fasting and weeping. And besides that disease at first by propagation, we have added to it by actual perpetration. We have increased our sickness, therefore sinners are said to wax worse and worse (2 Timothy 3:13).

2. Sin may be resembled to sickness for the nature of it.
Firstly, sickness is of a spreading nature, it spreads all over the body, it works into every part, the head and stomach, and it disorders the whole body. So sin doth not rest in one part, but spreads into all the faculties of the soul and members of the body: '... the whole head is sick, and the whole heart faint. From the sole of the foot even unto the head, there is no soundness in it; but wounds and bruises, and putrefying sores' (Isaiah 1:5, 6).

Sin doth corrupt the *understanding*. Gregory Nazianzene calls the understanding the lamp of reason. This lamp burns dim: 'Having their understanding darkened' (Ephesians 4:18); sin hath drawn a veil over the understanding, it hath cast a mist before our eyes, that we neither know God nor ourselves. Naturally we are only wise to do evil (Jeremiah 4:22). Witty at sin, wise to damn ourselves; the understanding becomes defiled. We can no more judge of spiritual objects till the Spirit of God anoint our eyes, than a blind man can judge of colours; our understandings are subject to mistakes; 'we call evil good, and good evil; we put bitter for sweet, and sweet for bitter' (Isaiah 5:20). A straight stick under water seems crooked; so to a natural understanding the straight line of truth seems crooked.

The *memory* is diseased. The memory at first was like a golden cabinet in which divine truths were locked up safe, but now it is like a colander or leaking vessel, which lets all that is good run out. The memory is like a searcer, which sifts out the flour, but keeps the bran. So the memory lets saving truths go, and holds nothing but froth and vanity. Many a man can remember a story, when he hath forgot his creed. Thus the memory is diseased; the memory is like a bad stomach that wants the retentive faculty, all the meat comes up again: so the most precious truths will not stay in the memory, but are gone again.

The *will* is diseased. The will is the soul's commander-in-chief, it is the master-wheel; but how irregular and eccentric is it! The will in the creation was like that golden bridle which Minerva was said to put upon Pegasus to guide and rule him; it did answer to God's will. This was the language of the will in innocency, 'I delight to do thy will, O God' (Psalm 40:8). But now it is distempered, like an iron sinew that refuseth to yield and bend to God (Isaiah 48:4); 'Ye will not come to me, that ye might have life' (John 5:40). Men will rather die than come to their physician. The Arminians talk of free will; but the will is sick, and what freedom hath a sick man to walk; the will is a rebel against God: 'Ye do always resist the Holy Ghost' (Acts 7:51). The will is diseased.

The *affections* are sick in three ways. Firstly, the affection of *desire*; a sick man desires that which is hurtful for him, he calls for wine in a fever. So the natural man being sick, he desires that which is prejudicial for him; he hath no desire after Christ, he doth not hunger and thirst after righteousness; but he desires poison, he desires to take his fill of sin, he loves death (Proverbs 8:36).

Secondly, the affection of *grief*; a man grieves for the want of an estate, but not for the want of God's favour: he grieves to see the plague or cancer in his body, but not for the plague of his heart.

Thirdly, the affection of *joy*; many can rejoice in a wedge of gold, not in the cross of Christ. The affections are sick and distempered.

The conscience is *diseased*: 'Their mind and conscience is defiled' (Titus 1:15). Conscience is either *erroneous*, binding to that which is sinful (John 16:2); 'I verily thought with myself I ought to do many things contrary to the name of Jesus' (Acts 26:9). Conscience is an *ignis fatuus*, leading out of the right way. Or *dumb*, it will not tell men of sin; it is a silenced preacher. Or, *dead* (Ephesians 4:19). Conscience is stupefied and senseless; the custom of sinning hath taken away the sense of sinning. Thus the sickness of sin hath gone over the whole soul, like that cloud which overspread the face of the heavens (1 Kings 18:45).

Secondly, sickness doth debilitate and weaken the body; a sick man is unfit to walk; so this sickness of sin weakens the soul: 'When we were without strength Christ died' (Romans 5:6). In innocency Adam was, in some sense, like the angels, he could serve God with a winged swiftness, and filial cheerfulness; but sin brought sickness into the soul, and this sickness hath cut the lock where his strength lay; he is now disarmed of all ability for service; and where grace is wrought, though a Christian be not so heartsick as before, yet he is very faint. The saints' prayers do but whisper in God's ears, and if Christ did not pray them over again, God could not hear them. We sin fervently, but pray faintly, as David said in 2 Samuel 3:39: 'I am this day weak, though anointed king'. Christians, though they have the oil of grace poured upon them, and they are anointed spiritual kings, yet they are weak: sin hath enfeebled them; they take their breath short, and cannot put forth such strong desires after God as they ought. When we find ourselves dead in duty, our holy affections languishing, think thus, This is my sickness, sin hath made me weak; as Jephthah said to his daughter:, 'Alas my daughter, thou hast brought me very low' (Judges 11:35); so may the soul say, Alas, my sin, thou hast brought me very low, thou hast brought me almost to the gates of death.

3. *Sickness doth eclipse the beauty of the body.*
This I ground on that Scripture, Psalm 39:11, 'When thou with rebukes dost correct man for iniquity, thou makest his beauty to consume away like a moth.' The moth consumes the beauty of the cloth; so a fit of sickness consumes the beauty of the body. Thus sin is a soul-sickness, it hath eclipsed the glory and splendour of the soul, it hath turned ruddiness into paleness; that beauty of grace which once sparkled as gold, now it may be said, 'How is this gold become dim!' (Lamentations 4:1). That soul which once had an orient brightness in it was more ruddy than rubies, its polishing of sapphire, the understanding bespangled with knowledge, the will crowned with liberty, the affections like so many seraphim burning in love to God, now the glory is departed. Sin hath turned beauty into deformity; as some faces by sickness are so disfigured, and look so ghastly, they can hardly be known:

so the soul of man is by sin so sadly metamorphosed (having lost the image of God) that it can hardly be known. 'The sun shall be turned into darkness' (Joel 2:31). Sin hath turned that sun of beauty which shined in the soul into a Cimmerian darkness; and where grace is begun to be wrought, yet the soul's beauty is not quite recovered, but is like the sun under a cloud.

4. Sickness takes away the taste.
A sick man doth not taste that sweetness in his meat; so the sinner by reason of soul-sickness, hath lost his taste for spiritual things. The Word of God is *pabulum animae*, it is bread to strengthen, wine to comfort; but the sinner tastes no sweetness in the Word. A child of God who is spiritualised by grace tastes a savouriness in ordinances, the promise drops as an honey-comb (Psalm 19:10). But a natural man is sick, and his taste is gone; since the tasting of the forbidden tree, he hath lost his taste.

5. Sickness takes away the comfort of life.
A sick person hath no joy of any thing, his life is a burden to him. So the sin-sick soul is void of all true comfort, and his laughter is but the pleasing dream of a sick man. He hath no true title to comfort, his sin is not pardoned, he may be in hell before tonight for any thing he knows.

6. Sickness ushers in death.
It is the prologue to death. Sickness is as it were the cutting of the tree, and death is the falling of the tree. This disease of sin (if not cured in time) brings the second death.

What the diseases of the soul are
Adam by breaking the box of original righteousness hath filled the soul full of diseases; the body is not subject to so many diseases as the soul: I cannot reckon them all up. 'Who can understand his errors?' (Psalm 19:12). Only I shall name some of the worst of these diseases. Pride is the tympany of the soul, lust

is the fever, error the gangrene, unbelief the plague of the heart, hypocrisy the scurvy, hardness of heart the stone, anger the phrenzy, malice the wolf in the breast, covetousness the dropsy, spiritual sloth the green sickness, apostasy the epilepsy; here are eleven soul-diseases, and when they come to the full height they are dangerous, and most frequently prove mortal.

Sin is the worst sickness

To have a body full of plague sores is sad; but to have the soul, which is the more noble part, spotted with sin, and full of the tokens, is far worse; as appears:

(1) The body may be diseased, and the conscience quiet. 'The inhabitant of the land shall not say I am sick' (Isaiah 33:24). He should scarce feel his sickness because sin was pardoned. But when the soul is sick of any reigning lust, the conscience is troubled: 'There is no peace to the wicked, saith my God' (Isaiah 57:21). When Spira had abjured his former faith, he was put *in little ease*, his conscience burned as hell, and no spiritual physic that divines did apply could ever allay that inflammation.

(2) A man may have bodily diseases, yet God may love him. 'Asa was diseased in his feet' (1 Kings 15:23). He had the gout, yet he was a favourite with God. God's hand may go out against a man, yet his heart may be towards him; diseases are the arrows which God shoots; pestilence is called God's arrow (Psalm 91:5). This arrow, as Gregory Nazianzene saith, may be sent from the hand of an indulgent father: but soul diseases are symptoms of God's anger, as he is a holy God, he cannot but hate sin, 'he beholds the proud afar off' (Psalm 138:6). God hates a sinner for his plaguesores: 'My soul loathed them' (Zechariah 11:8).

(3) Sickness, at worst, doth but separate from the society of friends; but this disease of sin, if not cured, separates from the society of God and angels. The leper was to be shut out of the camp; the leprosy of sin, without the interposition of mercy, shuts men out of the camp of heaven (Revelation 21:8). This is the misery of them that die in their sins, they are allowed neither

friend nor physician to come at them, they are excluded God's presence for ever, in whose presence is fullness of joy.

Use 1. Information

See into what a sad condition sin hath brought us; it hath made us desperately sick; nay, we die away in our sickness, till we are fetched again with the water of life. O how many sick bedrid souls are there in the world! Sick of pride, sick of lust; sin hath turned our houses and churches into hospitals, they are full of sick persons. What David's enemies said reproachfully of him, is true of every natural man: 'An evil disease cleaveth fast unto him' (Psalm 41:8). He hath the 'plague of the heart'. And even those who are regenerate are cured but in part, they have some grudgings of the disease, some ebullitions and stirrings of corruption. Nay, sometimes the king's evil breaks forth to the scandal of religion, and from this sin-sickness ariseth all other diseases, plague, gout, stone, and fever. 'He that eateth and drinketh unworthily, eateth and drinketh damnation to himself; for this cause many are weak and sickly among you' (1 Corinthians 11:29, 30).

If sin be a soul-sickness, then how foolish are they that hide their sins; it is folly to hide a disease! 'If I covered my transgression as Adam, by hiding my iniquity in my bosom ... let thistle grow instead of wheat' (Job 31:33, 40). The wicked take more care to have sin covered than cured; if they can but sin in private and not be suspected, they think all is well; there is a curse belongs to him who puts sin in a secret place (Deuteronomy 27:15). The hiding and concealing a disease proves mortal. 'He that covereth his sins, shall not prosper' (Proverbs 28:13).

If sin be a soul-sickness, then what need is there of the ministry? Ministers are physicians under God to cure sick souls; God hath set in his church pastors and teachers (Ephesians 4:11). The ministers are a college of physicians, their work is to find out diseases and apply medicines; it is a hard work, while ministers are curing others, they themselves are nigh unto death (Philippians 2:30). They find their people sick of several diseases; some have poisoned themselves with error, some are surfeited with the love of the creature, some have stabbed themselves at the heart with gross sin. O how hard is it to heal all these sick gangrened souls! Many ministers do sooner kill themselves by preaching than cure their patients; but though the work of the ministry be a laborious work, it is a needful work; while there are sick souls, there will be need of spiritual physicians.

How unworthy then are they who malign and persecute the ministers of God! (1 Corinthians 4:9). O unkind world, thus to use thy physician; can there be a greater injury to souls? Would it not be a piece of the highest cruelty and barbarism, if there were an act made that all physicians should be banished out of the land? And is it not worse to see multitudes of sick souls lie bleeding, and to have their spiritual physicians removed from them, which should under God heal them? This is a wrath-procuring sin: 'They misused his prophets, until the wrath of the LORD arose against his people, till there was no remedy' (2 Chronicles 36:16). See what is inscribed in Levi's blessing in Deuteronomy 33:8, 11: 'And of Levi he said, let thy Thummim and thy Urim be with thy holy one ... Bless, LORD, his substance, and accept the work of his hands; smite through the loins of them that rise against him, and of them that hate him, that they rise not again.' The Lord will wither that arm which is stretched out against his prophets.

Use 2. Exhort
If sin be a soul-disease, let this serve to *humble* us; the scripture often calls upon us to humility (1 Peter 5:5); if any thing will humble, this consideration may; sin is a soul-disease. If a woman had a fair face, but a cancer in her breast, it would keep her from being proud of her beauty. So Christian, though thou art endued with knowledge and morality, which are fair to look upon, yet remember thou art diseased in thy soul, here is a cancer in the breast to humble thee; this certainly is one reason why God leaves

sin in his own children; (for though sin be healed as to the guilt of it, yet not as to the stain of it) that the sight of their sores may make their plumes of pride fall.

There are two humbling sights; a sight of God's glory, and a sight of our diseases. Uzziah the king had no cause to be proud; for though he had a crown of gold on his head, he had the leprosy in his forehead (2 Chronicles 26:19). Though the saints have their golden graces, yet they have their leprous spots; seeing sin hath made us vile, let it make us humble; seeing it hath taken away our beauty, let it take away our pride; if God (saith Austin) did not spare the proud angels, will he spare thee, who art but dust and rottenness? O look upon your boils and ulcers, and be humble! Christians are never more lovely in God's eyes, than when they are loathsome in their own; those sins which humble, shall never damn.

If sin be a soul-disease, and the most damnable disease, let us be *afraid* of it. Had we diseases in our bodies, an ulcer in the lungs, or hectic fever, we would fear lest they should bring death; O fear sin-sickness, lest it bring the second death. Thou who art a drunkard or a swearer, tremble at thy soul maladies. I wonder to see sinners like the leviathan, made without fear. Why do not men fear sin? Why do they not shake with this disease?

The first reason is *stupidity*; as they have the fever of sin, so withal a lethargy: 'Having their conscience seared with a hot iron' (1 Timothy 4:2). He that hath an unbelieving heart and a seared conscience, you may ring out the bell; for that man's case is desperate.

A second reason is *presumption*. Many fancy that they can lay a fig upon the boil; though they be sick, they can make themselves well; it is but saying a few prayers, it is but a sigh or a tear, and they shall presently recover. But is it so easy to be healed of sin? Is it easy to make old Adam bleed to death? Is it easy when the pangs of death are on thee, in an instant to have the pangs of the new birth? O take heed of a spiritual lethargy! Fear your disease, lest it prove mortal and damnable. Physicians tell of a disease that makes men die laughing; so Satan tickles many with the pleasure of sin, and they die laughing.

If sin be a soul distemper, then *account them your best friends that would reclaim you from your sins*. The patient is thankful to the physician that tells him of his disease, and useth means to recover him. When ministers tell you, in love, of your sins, and would reclaim you, take it in good part; the worst they intend is to cure you of your sickness. David was glad of a healing reproof: 'Let the righteous smite me; it shall be a kindness: and let him reprove me; it shall be an excellent oil which shall not break my head' (Psalm 141:5). Ministers are charged by virtue of their office to reprove (2 Timothy 4:2). They must as well come with corrosives as lenitives: 'Wherefore rebuke them sharply, that they may be sound in the faith' (Titus 1:13).

The Greek word is cuttingly; as a surgeon searcheth a wound and then lanceth, and cuts out the gangrened flesh; or as a physician useth leeches and cupping glasses, which put the patient in pain, but it is to restore him to health; so must the ministers of Christ rebuke sharply that they may help to save their dying patients. Who is angry with the physician for prescribing a bitter potion? Why should any be angry with Christ's ministers for reproving, when in regard of their office they are physicians, and in regard of their bowels they are fathers? But how few are they who will take a reproof kindly! 'They hate him that rebuketh in the gate' (Amos 5:10). But why do not men love a reproof?

Firstly, because they are in *love* with their sins. A strange thing that any should love their disease, but so it is. 'How long, ye simple ones, will ye love simplicity?' (Proverbs 1:22). Sin is the poison of the soul, yet men love it; and he who loves his sin, hates a reproof.

Secondly, sin possesseth men with a *lunacy*. People are mad in sin. When sickness grows so violent that men lie raving, and are mad, they then quarrel with their physician, and say he comes to kill them. So when sin is grown to a head, the disease turned to a phrenzy, then men quarrel with those that tell them of their sins, and are ready to offer violence to their physicians. It argues wisdom to receive a reproof. 'Rebuke a wise man, and he will love thee' (Proverbs 9:8,). A wise man had rather drink a sharp potion, than die of his disease.

If sin be a soul-sickness, then do not *feed this disease*. He that is wise, will avoid those things which will increase his disease; if he be feverish, he will avoid wine which would inflame the disease; if he have the stone, he will avoid salt meats; he will forbear a dish he loves, because it is bad for his disease. Why should not men be as wise for their souls? Thou that hast a drunken lust, do not feed it with wine; thou that hast a malicious lust, do not feed it with revenge; thou that hast an unclean lust, make not provision for the flesh (Romans 13:14). He that feeds a disease, feeds an enemy. Some diseases are starved. Starve thy sins by fasting and humiliation. Either kill thy sin, or thy sin will kill thee.

If sin be a soul-disease, and worse than any other, then *labour to be sensible of this disease*. There are few who are sensible of their soul-sickness; they think they are well and ail nothing; that they are whole and need not a physician. It is a bad symptom to hear a sick dying man say he is well. The church of Laodicea was a sick patient, but she thought she was well (Revelation 3:17). Come to many a man and feel his pulse, ask him about the state of his soul, he will say, he hath a good heart, and doubts not but he shall be saved. What should be the reason that when men are so desperately sick in their souls, and ready to drop into hell, yet they conceit themselves in a very good condition?

Firstly, there is a *spiritual cataract* upon their eye, they see not their sores. Laodicea thought herself rich, because she was blind (Revelation 3:17). The god of this world blinds men's eyes that they can neither see their disease nor their physician. Many bless God their estate is good, not from the knowledge of their happiness, but from the ignorance of their danger; when Haman's face was covered, he was near execution. Oh pray with David, 'Lighten mine eyes, that I sleep not the sleep of death' (Psalm 13:3).

Secondly, men that are sick think themselves well, from the *haughtiness* of their spirits. Alexander thought himself a while to be the son of Jupiter, and no less than a god. What an arrogant creature is man! Though he be sick unto death, he thinks it too much a disparagement to acknowledge a disease; either he is not sick, or he can heal himself. If he be poisoned, he runs to the herb, or rather weed, of his own righteousness to cure him.

Thirdly, men that are sick conceit themselves well, through *self-love*. He that loves another will not credit any evil report of him. Men are self-lovers (2 Timothy 3:2). Every man is a dove in his own eye, therefore doth not suspect himself of any disease. He will rather question the Scripture's verity than his own malady.

Fourthly, *self-deceit* and the deceit of the heart appear in two things. First, in *hiding the disease*; the heart hides sin as Rachel did her father's images (Genesis 31:34). Hazael did not think he was so sick as he was; he could not imagine that so much wickedness, like a disease, should lie lurking in him: 'Is thy servant a dog, that he should do this great thing?' (2 Kings 8:13). As the viper hath his teeth hid in his gums, so that if one should look into his mouth he would think it a harmless creature; so though there be much corruption in the heart, yet the heart hides it, and draws a veil over, that it be not seen. Second, the heart holds a false glass before the eye, making a man appear fair, and his estate very good. The heart can *deceive with counterfeit grace*. Hence it is that men are insensible of their spiritual condition, and think themselves well when they are sick unto death.

Fifthly, men take up a reverend opinion of themselves, and fancy their spiritual estate better than it is, through mistake. And this mistake is double.

To begin with, they *enjoy glorious privileges*; they were born within the sound of Aaron's bells, they were baptized with holy water, they have been fed with manna from heaven; therefore they hope they are in a good condition: 'Then Micah said, Now I know the LORD will do me good, seeing I have a Levite to my priest' (Judges 17:13). But alas! this is a mistake; outward privileges save not. What is any man the better for the ordinances, unless he be the better by the ordinances? A child may die with the breast in its mouth. Many of the Jews perished, though Christ himself was their preacher.

The other mistake is set down by the apostle in 2 Corinthians 10:12: 'They, measuring themselves by themselves, and comparing themselves amongst themselves, are not wise.' Here is a double error, or mistake. First, 'They measure themselves *by* themselves': that is, they see they are not so bad as they were, therefore they judge their condition is good. A dwarf may be taller than he was, yet a dwarf still; the patient may be less sick than he was, yet far from well; a man may be better than he was, yet not good.

Then 'they compare themselves *amongst* themselves.' They see they are not so flagitious and profane as others; therefore they think themselves well, because they are not so sick as others: this is a mistake, one may as well die of a consumption as the plague. One man may not be so far off heaven as another, yet he may not be near heaven; one line may not be so crooked as another, yet not straight. To the law, to the testimony; the word of God is the true standard and measure by which we are to judge of the state and temper of our souls.

Oh let us take heed of this rock, the fancying of our condition better than it is; let us take heed of a spiritual apoplexy, to be sick in our souls, yet not sensible of this sickness. What do men talk of a light within them? The light within them by nature is not sufficient to show them the diseases of their souls; for this light tells them they are whole, and have no need of a physician.

Oh what infinite mercy is it for a man to be made sensible of sin, and seeing himself sick, to cry out with David in 2 Samuel

12:13, 'I have sinned against the LORD.' Were it not a mercy for a person that is distracted, to be restored to the use of his reason; so for him that is spiritually distempered, and in a lethargy, to come to himself, and see both his wound and his remedy: till the sinner be sensible of his disease, the medicine of mercy doth not belong to him.

If sin be a soul sickness, then *labour to get this disease healed*. If a man had a disease in his body, a pleurisy or cancer, he would use all the means for a cure; the woman in the gospel who had a bloody issue, spent her whole estate upon the physicians (Luke 8:43). Be more earnest to have thy soul cured than thy body. Use David's prayer in Psalm 41:4: 'Heal my soul for I have sinned.' Hast thou a consumptive body, rather pray God to heal the consumption in thy soul; go to God first for the cure of thy soul. In James 5:14, we are told, 'Is any sick among you? let him call for the elders of the church, and let them pray over him'. The writer doth not say, let him call for the physician, but the elders, that is, the ministers. Physicians are to be consulted in their due place, but not in the first place. Most men send first for the physician, and then for the minister; which shows they are more desirous and careful for the recovery of their bodies than their souls. But if soul diseases are more dangerous and deadly, then we should prefer the spiritual cure before the bodily; 'Heal my soul, for I have sinned'; let us consider the following:

Till we are cured, we are not fit to do God any service. A sick man cannot work; while the disease of sin is violent, we are not fit for any heavenly employment; we can neither work for God nor work out our salvation. The philosopher defines happiness as the operation of the mind about virtue. To be working for God is both the end of our life, and the perfection. Would we be active in our sphere? Let us labour to have our souls cured. So long as we are diseased with sin, we are lame and bed-rid, we are unfit for work. We read indeed of a sinner's works, but they are dead works (Hebrew 6:1).

If we are not cured, we are cursed; if our diseases abide on us, the wrath of God abides on us.

But how shall we get this disease of sin cured? This brings us to the second thing in the text - the healing physician.

2. Jesus Christ is a soul-physician

Ministers (as was said before) are physicians, whom Christ doth in his name delegate, and send abroad into the world. He saith to the apostles, and in them to all his ministers, 'Lo, I am with you alway, even unto the end of the world' (Matthew 28:20). That is, I am with you to assist and bless you, and to make your ministry healing; but though ministers are physicians, yet but under-physicians. Jesus Christ is the chief physician; he it is that teacheth us all our receipts, and goes forth with our labours, else the physic we prescribe would never work; all the ministers under heaven would not do any cure without the help of this great physician. For the amplification of this I shall show: (1) That Christ is a physician; (2) Why he is a physician; (3) That he is the only physician; (4) How he heals his patients; (5) That he is the best physician.

1. Christ is a physician

It is one of his titles: 'I am the LORD that healeth thee' (Exodus 15:26). He is a physician for the body; he 'anointed the blind, cleansed the lepers, healed the sick, raised the dead' (Matthew 11:5). He it is that puts virtue into physic, and makes it healing. And he is a physician for the soul: 'He healeth the broken in heart' (Psalm 147:3). We are all as so many impotent, diseased persons; one man hath a fever, another a dead palsy, another hath a bloody issue, he is under the power of some hereditary corruption. Now Christ is a soul-physician, for he healeth these diseases. Therefore in Scripture, the Lord Jesus, to set forth his healing virtue, is resembled:

(1) By the brazen serpent (Numbers 21:9). Those who were stung, were cured by looking on the brazen serpent; so when the

soul is stung by the old serpent, it is cured by that healing under Christ's wings.

(2) By the good Samaritan in Luke 10:30-35. We have wounded ourselves by sin, and the wound had been incurable, had not Christ, that good Samaritan, poured in wine and oil.

(3) By the trees of the sanctuary: 'The fruit thereof shall be for meat, and the leaf thereof shall be for medicine' (Ezekiel 47:12). Thus the Lord Jesus, that tree of life in paradise, hath a sanative virtue; he heals our pride, unbelief etc. As he feeds our graces, so he heals our corruptions.

2. Why Christ is a physician

(1) In regard of his call; God the Father called him to practise physic, he anointed him to the work of healing: 'The Spirit of the Lord is upon me, because he hath anointed me to preach the gospel: he hath sent me to heal the broken-hearted' (Luke 4:18). Christ came into the world as into an hospital, to heal sin-sick souls: this, though it was a glorious work, yet Christ would not undertake it, till he was commissioned by his Father. 'The Spirit of the Lord is upon me, he hath sent me.' Christ was anointed and appointed to the work of a physician, this was for our imitation; we are not to meddle many matters without a call; that is acting out of our sphere.

(2) Jesus Christ undertook this healing work, because of that need we were in of a physician. Christ came to be our physician, not because we deserved him, but because we needed him; not our merit, but our misery, drew Christ from heaven; had he not come, we must of necessity have perished, and died of our wounds; our disease was not ordinary, it had seized on every part; it made us not only sick but dead; and such receipts were necessary as none but Christ could give.

(3) Christ came as a physician out of the sweetness of his nature; he is like the good Samaritan, who had compassion on the wounded man (Luke 10:33). A physician may come to the patient only for gain; not so much to help the patient as to help himself:

but Christ came purely out of sympathy; there was nothing in us to tempt Christ to heal us; for we had no desire of a physician, nor had we any thing to give our physician; as sin made us sick, so it made us poor; so that Christ came as a physician, not out of hope to receive any thing from us, but was prompted to it out of his own goodness: 'I will heal their backslidings, I will love them freely' (Hosea 14:4). Love set Christ a work; not only his Father's commission, but his own compassion moved him to his spiritual physic and chirurgery. King David banished the blind and lame out of the city (2 Samuel 5:8). Christ comes to the blind and lame, and cures them; it is the sounding of his bowels that causeth the healing under his wings.

3. Christ is the only physician

'Neither is there salvation in any other' (Acts 4:12). There is no other physician besides. The papists would have other healers besides Christ, they would make angels their physicians; all the angels in heaven cannot heal one sick soul; indeed they are described by their wings (Isaiah 6:2), but they have no healing under their wings. Papists would heal themselves by their own merits. Adam did eat that apple which made him and his posterity sick; but he could not find any herb in paradise to cure him; our merits are rather damning than healing; to make use of other physicians and medicines, is as if the Israelites, in contempt of that brazen serpent which Moses set up, had erected other brazen serpents. O let us take heed of that *turba medicorum*.

Indeed in bodily sickness it is lawful to multiply physicians; when the patient hath advised with one physician, he desires to have others joined with him; but the sick soul, if it joins any other physician with Christ it surely dies.

4. How Christ heals his patients

There are four things in Christ that are healing.

1. His *Word* is healing: 'He sent his word, and healed them' (Psalm 107:20). His Word in the mouth of his ministers is

healing; when the spirit is wounded in desertion, Christ doth create the lips that speak peace (Isaiah 57:19). The Word written is a repository in which God hath laid up sovereign oils and balsams to recover sick souls; and the word preached is the pouring out of these oils, and applying them to the sick patient. 'He sent his word and healed them.' We look upon the word as a weak thing. What is the breath of a man to save a soul? But 'The power of the Lord is present to heal' (Luke 5:17). Christ makes use of his word as a healing medicine; the receipts which his ministers prescribe, he himself applies; he makes his word convincing, converting, comforting.

Caution: not that the word heals all; to some it is not a healing but a killing word: 'To the one we are a savour of death unto death' (2 Corinthians 2:16). Some die of their disease; two sorts of patients die. Such as sin *presumptuously*; though they know a thing to be sin: they are of those that rebel against the light (Job 24:13); this is dangerous. David prays in Psalm 19:13: 'Keep back thy servant from presumptuous sins.' Such as sin *maliciously*; when the disease comes to this head, the patient will die (Hebrews 10:29). But to them who belong to the election of grace, the word is the healing medicine Christ useth, 'He sent his word, and healed them.'

2. Christ's *wounds* are healing: 'with his stripes we are healed' (Isaiah 53:5). Christ made a medicine of his own body and blood; the physician died to cure the patient. The pelican when her young ones are bitten by serpents feeds them with her own blood to recover them. Thus when we were bitten by the old serpent, then Jesus Christ prescribes a receipt of his own blood to heal and restore us. The blood of Christ, being the blood of him who was God as well as man, had infinite merit to appease God, and infinite virtue to heal us: this is the balm of Gilead, that recovers a soul which is sick even unto death. Balm, as naturalists say, is a juice which a little shrub, being cut with glass, doth weep out. This was anciently of very precious esteem, the savour of it was odoriferous, the virtue of it sovereign; it would cure ulcers,

and the stinging of serpents. This balm may be an emblem of Christ's blood; it hath a most sovereign virtue in it, it heals the ulcer of sin, the stinging of tentation, and merits for us justification (Romans 5:9). O how precious is this balm of Gilead! By this blood we enter into heaven.

3. Christ's *Spirit* is healing; the blood of Christ heals the guilt of sin; the Spirit of Christ heals the pollution of sin; the Spirit is compared to oil, it is called the anointing of the Spirit (Isaiah 61:1) to show the healing virtue of the Spirit; for oil is healing. Christ by his Spirit heals the rebellion of the will, the stone of the heart; though sin be not removed, it is subdued.

4. Christ's *rod* is healing (Isaiah 27:9). Christ never wounds but to heal; the rod of affliction is to recover the sick patient. David's bones were broken that his soul might be healed. God useth affliction as the surgeon doth his lance, to let out the venom and corruption of the soul, and make way for a cure.

But if Christ be a physician, why are not all healed?
All are not healed, because all do not know they are sick; they see not the sores and ulcers of their souls; and will Christ cure them who see no need of him? Many ignorant people thank God they have good hearts; but that heart can no more be good which wants grace, than that body can be sound which wants health.

All are not healed, because they love their sickness: 'Thou lovest evil' (Psalm 52:3); many men hug their disease. Augustine saith, before his conversion, he prayed against sin, but his heart whispered, Not yet Lord; he was loath to leave his sin too soon; how many love their disease better than their physician! While sin is loved, Christ's medicines are loathed.

All are not healed, because they do not look out after a physician. If they have any bodily distemper upon them, they presently send to the physician; their souls are sick, but mind not their physician Christ: 'Ye will not come unto me that ye might have life' (John 5:40). Christ takes it as an undervaluing of him that we will not send to him. Some send for Christ when it is too late; when other physicians have given them over, and there is no hope of life, then they cry to Christ to save them, but Christ refuseth such patients as make use of him only for a shift; thou that scornest Christ in time of health, Christ may despise thee in the time of sickness.

All are not healed, because they would be self-healers; they would make their duties their saviours; the papists would be their own physicians; their daily sacrifice of the mass is a blasphemy against Christ's priestly office; but Christ will have the honour of the cure, or he will never heal us; not our tears, but his blood saves.

All are not healed, because they do not take the physic which Christ prescribes them; they would be cured, but they are loath to put themselves into a course of physic. Christ prescribes them to drink the bitter potion of repentance, and to take the pill of mortification, but they cannot do this, they had rather die than take physic. If the patient refuseth to take the receipts the physician prescribes, no wonder he is not healed. Christians, you have had many receipts to take, have you taken them? Ask your conscience. Many hearers of the word do like foolish patients, who send to the doctor for physic, but when they have it, they let the physic stand by in the glass, but do not take it; it is probable that you have not taken the receipts which the gospel prescribes, because the word hath no operation on your hearts, you are as proud, as earthly, as malicious as ever.

All are not healed, because they have not confidence in their physician; it is observable when Christ came to work any cure, he first put this question, 'Believe ye that I am able to do this?' (Matthew 9:28). This undoes many; O, saith the sinner, There is no mercy for me, Christ cannot heal me. Take heed, thy unbelief is worse than all thy other diseases. Did not Christ pray for them that crucified him? 'Father, forgive them!' Some of those were saved that had a hand in shedding his blood! (Acts 2:36, 37). Why then dost thou say Christ cannot heal thee? Unbelief dishonours Christ, it hinders from a cure, it closeth the orifice of Christ's wounds, it stauncheth his blood (Matthew 15:58). Millions die of their disease, because they do not believe in their physician.

5. Christ is the best physician
In order to set forth the praise and honour of Jesus Christ, I shall show you wherein he excels other physicians.

1. He is the most skilful physician; there is no disease too hard for him: 'Who healeth all thy diseases' (Psalm 103:3). The pool of Bethesda might be an emblem of Christ's blood: 'Whosoever first after the troubling of the water stepped in, was made whole of whatsoever disease he had' (John 5:5). There are certain diseases physicians cannot cure; as a consumption in the lungs, some kind of obstructions and gangrenes. Some diseases are the reproach of physicians, but there is no disease can pose Christ's skill; he can cure the gangrene of sin when it is come to the heart; he healed Mary Magdalene, an unchaste sinner; he healed Paul, who breathed out threatenings against the church; insomuch that Paul stands and wonders at the cure: 'But I obtained mercy' (1 Timothy 1:13); I was bemercied. Christ heals head distempers and heart distempers, which may keep poor trembling souls from despair. Oh, saith the sinner, never was any so diseased as I! But look up to thy physician Christ, who hath healing under his wings; he can melt a heart of stone, and wash away black sins in the crimson of his blood; there are no desperate cases with Christ; he hath those salves, oils and balsams which can cure the worst disease.

Indeed, there is one disease which Christ doth not heal, namely, the sin against the Holy Ghost; this is called 'a sin unto death'; if we knew any who had sinned this sin, we were to shut them out of our prayers: 'There is a sin unto death, I do not say that he shall pray for it' (1 John 5:16). There is no healing of this disease; not but that Christ could cure this, but the sinner will not be cured. The king could pardon a traitor, but if he will have no pardon he must die. The sin against the Holy Ghost is unpardonable, because the sinner will have no pardon; he scorns Christ's blood, despites his Spirit, therefore his sin hath no sacrifice (Hebrews 10:26-29).

2. Christ is the best physician, because he cures the better part, the soul; other physicians can cure the liver or spleen, Christ cures the heart; they can cure the blood when it is tainted, Christ cures the conscience when it is defiled: 'How much more shall the blood of Christ purge your conscience from dead works?' (Hebrews 9:14). Galen and Hippocrates might cure the stone in the kidneys, but Christ cures the stone in the heart; he is the best physician which cures the most excellent part. The soul is immortal, angelical; man was made in the image of God (Genesis 1:27). Not in regard of his body, but his soul. Now if the soul be so divine and noble, then the cure of the soul doth far exceed the cure of the body.

3. Christ is the best physician, for he causeth us to feel our disease. The disease of sin, though it be most damnable, yet is least discernible; many a man is sin-sick, but the devil hath given him such stupefying physic that he sleeps the sleep of death, and all the thunders of the world cannot awaken him. But the Lord Jesus, this blessed physician, awakes the soul out of its lethargy, and then it is in a hopeful way of recovery. The jailer was never so near a cure, as when he cried out, 'Sirs, what must I do to be saved?' (Acts 16:30).

4. Christ shows more love to his patients than any physician besides; this appears five ways:

(1) In that long journey he took from heaven to earth.

(2) In that he comes to his patients without sending for. The sick send to their physicians, and use many entreaties; here the physician comes unsent for: 'I am found of them that sought me not' (Isaiah 65:1). He comes to us with mercy, entreating us to be healed. If Christ had not first come to us, and like the good

Samaritan, poured in wine and oil, we must have died of our wounds.

(3) The physician lets himself bleed to cure his patient: 'But he was wounded for our transgressions' (Isaiah 53:5); through his wounds we may see his bowels.

(4) Our repulses and unkindnesses do not drive Christ away from us. Physicians, if provoked by their patients, go away in a rage, and will come no more. We abuse our physician, thrust him away, we bolt out our physician, yet Christ will not forsake us, but comes again, and applies his sovereign oils and balsams: 'I have spread out my hands all the day unto a rebellious people' (Isaiah 65:2). Christ puts up wrongs and incivilities, and is resolved to go through with the cure. O the love of this heavenly physician!

(5) Christ himself drank that bitter cup which we should have drunk; and by his taking the potion we are healed and saved. Thus Christ hath shown more love than ever physician did to the patient.

5. *Christ is the most cheap physician*: sickness is not only a consumption to the body but the purse (Mark 5:26). Physicians' fees are chargeable, but Jesus Christ gives us our physic freely, he takes no fee: 'Come without money and without price' (Isaiah 55:1). He desires us to bring nothing to him but broken hearts; and when he hath cured us he desires us to bestow nothing upon him but our love; and one would think that were very reasonable.

6. *Christ heals with more ease than any other*. Other physicians apply pills, potions and bleeding; but Christ cures with more facility. Christ made the devil go out with a word (Mark 9:25). So when the soul is spiritually possessed, Christ can with a word heal, nay, he can cure with a look. When Peter had fallen into a relapse, Christ looked on Peter, and he wept. Christ's look melted Peter into repentance; it was a healing look. If Christ doth but cast a look upon the soul, he can recover it. Therefore David prays to

have a look from God: 'Look thou upon me, and be merciful unto me' (Psalm 119:132).

7. *Christ is the most tender-hearted physician*. He hath ended his passion, yet not his compassion. How doth he pity sick souls! He is not more full of skill than sympathy: 'My heart is turned within me' (Hosea 11:8). Christ shows his compassion in that he doth proportion his physic to the strength of the patient. Physic, if it be too sharp for the constitution, endangers the life. Christ gives such gentle physic as works kindly and savingly. Though he will bruise sinners, yet 'he will not break the bruised reed.' O the soundings of Christ's bowels to poor souls that feel themselves heart-sick with sin! He holds their head and heart when they are fainting; he brings the cordials of his promises to keep the sick patient from dying away. Christians, you perhaps may have hard thoughts of your physician Christ, and think he is cruel, and intends to destroy you; but O the workings of his bowels towards humble broken-hearted sinners! 'He heals the broken in heart, and bindeth up their wounds' (Psalm 147:3). Every groan of the patient goes to the heart of this physician.

8. *Physicians often prescribe such physic as is prejudicial to the patient*, in two cases: Either in case they find not out the cause of the disease, and then they may give that which is contrary, such as hot things instead of cooling: or in case they do find out the cause, they may give that which is good for one thing and bad for another. As it falls out when the liver and spleen are both distempered, the physic which helps the liver may hurt the spleen. But Christ always prescribes that physic which is suitable, and withal he blesseth the physic. If the disease of the soul be pride, he humbles it with affliction. God turned Nebuchadnezzar to grass to cure him of his tympany. If the disease of the soul be sloth, Christ applies some awakening Scripture (Matthew 12:11; Luke 13:24; 1 Peter 4:18). If the disease be the stone of the heart, Christ useth proper medicines; sometimes the terrors of the law,

sometimes mercies, sometimes he dissolves the stone in his own blood. If the soul be fainting through unbelief, Christ brings some Scripture cordial to revive it: 'A bruised reed he will not break' (Matthew 12:20); 'I will not contend for ever, neither will I be always wroth: for the spirit should fail before me, and the souls which I have made' (Isaiah 57:16). Thus the Lord Jesus always prescribes that physic which is proper for the disease, and shall work effectually to the cure.

9. *Christ never fails of success.* Physicians may have skill, but not always success; patients often die under their hands; but Christ never undertakes to heal any but he makes a certain cure: 'Those that thou gavest me I have kept, and none of them is lost' (John 17:12). Judas was not given to Christ to be healed; but never any who was given to Christ did miscarry.

How shall I know that I am given to Christ to be cured?

If it be with thee as with a sick patient, who sees himself dying without a physician. Art thou undone without Christ? Dost thou perceive thyself bleeding to death without the balm of Gilead? Then thou art one of Christ's sick patients, and thou shalt never miscarry under his hands. How can any of those be lost whom Christ undertakes to cure? He pours out the perfume of his prayers for them as in John 17:11: 'Holy Father, keep through thy own name those whom thou hast given me.' Satan could never upbraid Christ with this, that any of his sick patients were lost.

10. *Other physicians can only cure them that are sick, but Christ cures them that are dead*: 'You hath he quickened who were dead in trespasses and sins' (Ephesians 2:1). A sinner hath all the signs of death on him; the pulse of his affections doth not beat, he is without breath, he breathes not after holiness. He is dead; but Christ is a physician for the dead; of every one whom Christ cures, it may be said, 'He was dead and is alive again' (Luke 15:32).

11. Christ cures not only our diseases, but our deformities. The physician can make the sick man well; but if he be deformed, he cannot make him fair. Christ gives not only health, but beauty. Sin hath made us ugly and misshapen; Christ's medicines do not only take away our sickness, but our spots; he doth not only make us whole, but fair: 'I will heal their backslidings'; 'His beauty shall be as the olive-tree' (Hosea 14:4,6). Jesus Christ never thinks he hath fully healed us, till he hath drawn his own beautiful image upon us. 'Arise, my fair one' (Canticles 2:13); fair with justification, fair with sanctification. Christ doth not only heal, but adorn; he is called the Sun of righteousness (Malachi 4:2) not only because of the healing under his wings, but because of those rays of beauty which he puts upon the soul (Revelation 12:1).

12. And lastly, Christ is the most bountiful physician. Other patients do enrich their physicians, but here the physician doth enrich the patient. Christ prefers all his patients; he doth not only cure them, but crown them (Revelation 2:10). Christ doth not only raise from the bed, but to the throne; he gives the sick man not only health, but heaven.

Use 1

Good news this day, there is balm in Gilead; there is a physician to heal sin-sick souls. The angels that fell had no physician sent them, we have. There are but few in the world to whom Christ is revealed; they that have the gold of the Indies want the blood of the Lamb. But the Sun of righteousness is risen in our hemisphere, with healing in his wings.

If a man were poisoned, what a comfort would it be to him to hear that there was an herb in the garden that could heal him! If he had a gangrene in his body, and were given over by all his friends, how glad would he be to hear of a surgeon that could cure him! O sinner, thou art full of peccant humours, thou hast a gangrened soul; but there is a physician that can recover thee. 'There is hope in Israel concerning this'; though there be an old serpent to sting us with his tentations, yet there is a brazen serpent to heal us with his blood.

Use 2

If Christ be a physician, then let us make use of this physician for our diseased souls: 'When the sun was setting, all they that had any sick with divers diseases, brought them unto him, and he laid his hands on every one of them and healed them' (Luke 4:40). You that have neglected a physician all this while, now when the sun of the gospel, and the sun of your life is even setting, bring your sick souls to Christ to be cured. Christ complains that though men are sick even to death, yet they will not come or send to the physician: 'Ye will not come to me that ye might have life' (John 5:40). In bodily diseases the physician is the first that is sent to; in soul diseases the Physician is the last that is sent to. But here there are many sad objections that poor souls make against themselves, why they do not come to Christ their soul physician.

Objections

Alas, I am discouraged to go to Christ to cure me, because of my unworthiness; just like the centurion, who sent to Christ about his sick servant: 'Lord, trouble not thyself, for I am not worthy that thou shouldest enter under my roof' (Luke 7:6).

Christ was coming to heal his servant, but the centurion would have staved off Christ from coming with 'I am not worthy'. So saith many a trembling soul, Christ is a physician, but who am I that Christ should come under my roof, or heal me? I am unworthy of mercy: as Mephibosheth said to King David: 'What is thy servant that thou shouldest look upon such a dead dog as I am?' (2 Samuel 9:8). Now to such as have their hearts broken with a sense of their unworthiness, and are discouraged from coming to Christ to heal them, let me say these five things by way of reply.

(1) Who did Christ shed his blood for but such as are unworthy? 'Jesus Christ came into the world to save sinners' (1

Timothy 1:14). Christ came into the world as into an hospital, among a company of lame, bed-rid souls.

(2) Though we are not legally worthy, we may be evangelically; it is part of our worthiness to see our unworthiness: 'Fear not, thou worm Jacob' (Isaiah 41:14). Thou mayest be a worm in thine own eye, yet a dove in God's eye.

(3) Though we are unworthy, yet Christ is worthy; we do not deserve a cure, but Christ hath merited mercy for us; he hath store of blood to supply our want of tears.

(4) Who was ever yet saved because he was worthy? What man could ever plead this title, Lord Jesus heal me, because I am worthy? What worthiness was in Paul before his conversion? What worthiness was there in Mary Magdalene, out of whom seven devils were cast? But free grace did pity and heal them; God doth not find us worthy, but makes us worthy.

(5) If we never come to Christ to be healed till we are worthy, we must never come: and let me tell you, this talking of worthiness savours of pride, we would have something of our own; had we such preparations and self-excellencies, then we think Christ would accept of us, and we might come and be healed; this is to fee our physician. O let not the sense of unworthiness discourage: go to Christ to be healed: 'Arise, he calleth thee' (Mark 10:49).

But I fear, I am not within Christ's commission, I am not of the number that shall be saved; and then though Christ be a physician, I shall not be healed.

We must take heed of drawing desperate conclusions against ourselves; it is high presumption for us to make ourselves wiser than the angels. All the angels in heaven are not able to resolve the question, Who are elected, and who are reprobated?

Thou that sayest thou art not within Christ's commission, read over Christ's commission, see who he comes to heal: 'He hath sent me to heal the broken-hearted' (Luke 4:18). Hath God touched thy heart with remorse? Dost thou weep more out of love to Christ, than fear of hell? Then thou art a broken-hearted sinner, and art within Christ's commission; a bleeding Christ will heal a broken heart.

But my sins are so many that sure I shall never be healed, I am sick of many diseases at once.

Thou hast the more need of a physician; one would think that was a strange speech from Peter to Christ: 'Depart from me, for I am a sinful man, O Lord' (Luke 5:8); rather, Lord, come near to me. Is it a good argument to say to a physician, I am diseased, therefore depart from me? No, therefore come and heal me. Our sins should serve to humble us, not to beat us from Christ. I tell you, if we had no diseases, Christ would have no work to do in the world.

But my disease is inflamed, and grown to a paroxysm; my sin is greatly heightened.

The plaster of Christ's blood is broader than thy sore: 'The blood of Jesus Christ cleanseth us from all sin' (1 John 1:7). The blood of the Lamb takes away the poison of the serpent: all diseases are alike to Christ's blood; he can cure the greatest sin as well as the least. Hast thou a bloody issue of sin running? The issue of blood in Christ's side can heal thine.

But mine is an old inveterate disease, and I fear it is incurable.

Though thy disease be chronical, Christ can heal it. Christ doth not say, if this disease had been taken in time, it might have been cured: he is good at old sores. The thief on the cross had an old festering disease, but Christ cured it; it was well for him his physician was so near. Zacchaeus, an old sinner, a custom-house man, had wronged many a man in his time, but Christ cured him. Christ sometimes grafts his grace upon an old stock; we read Christ cured at sunsetting (Luke 4:40). He heals some sinners at the sunsetting of their lives.

*But after I have been healed, my disease hath broken out again;
I have relapsed into the same sin; therefore I fear there is no
healing for me.*

It is rare that the Lord leaves his children to these relapses,
though, through the suspension of grace, and the prevalency of
temptation, it is possible they might fall back into sin; these sins
of relapse are sad. It was an aggravation of Solomon's offence,
that he sinned after the Lord had appeared to him twice (1 Kings
11:9). These sins after healing open the mouth of conscience to
accuse, and stop the mouth of God's Spirit, which should speak
peace. These sins exclude from the comfort of the promise; it is
as it were sequestrated; but if the soul be deeply humbled, if the
relapsing sinner be a relenting sinner, let him not cast away the
anchor of hope, but have recourse to his soul-physician; Jesus
Christ can cure a relapse, he healed David's and Cranmer's
relapse.

'If any man sin, we have an advocate with the Father, Jesus
Christ' (1 John 2:1). Christ appears in the court as the advocate
for the client. As he poured out his blood upon the brazen altar of
the cross: so he pours out his prayers at the golden altar in heaven:
'He ever liveth to make intercession for us' (Hebrews 7:25).
Christ, in the golden work of intercession, presents the merit of
his blood to his Father, and so obtains our pardon, and applies the
virtue of his blood to us, and so works our cure; therefore be not
discouraged from going to thy physician; though thy disease hath
broken out again, yet Christ hath fresh sprinklings of his blood
for thee, he can cure a relapse.

*But there is no healing for me, I fear I have sinned the sin against
the Holy Ghost?*

Firstly, the fear of sinning it, is a sign thou hast not sinned it.

Secondly, let me ask, Why dost thou think thou hast sinned
the sin against the Holy Ghost? Thou sayest, I have grieved the
Spirit of God.

Every grieving the Spirit of God is not that fatal sin. We grieve the Spirit when we sin against the illumination of it; the Spirit being grieved, may depart for a time, and carry away all his honey out of the hive, leaving the soul in darkness (Isaiah 50:10). But every grieving the Spirit is not the sin against the Holy Ghost. A child of God when he hath sinned, his heart smites him; and he whose heart smites him for sin hath not committed the unpardonable sin. A child of God having grieved the Spirit, doth as Noah when the dove did fly out of the ark, he opened the windows of the ark to let it in again. A godly man doth not shut his heart against the Spirit, as a wicked man doth (Acts 7:51). The Spirit of God would come in, he keeps him out; but a gracious soul opens his heart to let in the Spirit, as Noah opened the door of the ark to let in the dove. Christian, is it not so with thee? Then be of good comfort, thou hast not sinned the sin against the Holy Ghost; that sin is a malicious despiting of the Spirit, which thou tremblest to think of.

Therefore, laying aside these arguments and disputes, whatever the diseases of the soul are, come to Christ for a cure, believe in his blood, and thou mayest be saved? You see what a skilful and able physician Christ is, what sovereign oils and balsams he hath, how willing he is to cure sick souls. O then what remains, but that you cast yourselves upon his merits to heal and save you!

Of all sins unbelief is the worst, because it casts disparagement on Christ, as if he were not able to work a cure. O Christian, believe in thy physician, for ' whosoever believeth in him shall not perish' (John 3:16). Say as Queen Esther, 'I will go in unto the king, which is not according to the law, and if I perish, I perish' (Esther 4:16). So say, The Lord Jesus is a physician to heal me, I will adventure on his blood, if I perish, I perish. Queen Esther ventured against the law, she had no promise that the king would hold out the golden sceptre; but I have a promise which invites me to come to Christ: 'He that comes unto me I will in no wise cast him out' (John 6:37). Faith is a healing grace: we read, when the Israelites were burying a man, for fear of the soldiers of the Moabites, they cast him for haste into the grave of Elisha; now the man, as soon as he was down, and had touched the dead body of the prophet, revived, and stood up on his feet (2 Kings 13:21). So if a man be dead in sin, yet let him be cast in Christ's grave, and by faith touch Christ, who was dead and buried, he will revive, and his soul will be healed.

Remember there is no way for a cure but by believing; Christ himself will not avail us: 'Whom God hath set forth to be a propitiation through faith in his blood' (Romans 3:25). Faith is the applying of Christ's merits. A plaster, though it be ever so rare and excellent, yet if it be not applied to the wound, will do no good; though the plaster be made of Christ's blood, yet it will not heal, unless applied by faith. The brazen serpent was a sovereign remedy for the cure of those that were stung; but if they had not looked upon it, they received no benefit. So though there be a healing virtue in Christ, yet unless we look upon him by the eye of faith, we cannot be cured. Above all things labour for faith; this is the all-healing grace; this hand touching Christ fetches virtue from him.

Not that faith hath more worthiness than other graces; but only it is influential, as it makes us one with Christ. If a man had a stone in a ring that could cure many diseases, we say this ring heals; but it is not the ring, but the stone in the ring that doth the cure; so faith saves and heals, not by its own virtue, but as it lays hold on Christ, and fetches down his sacred influences into the soul.

If Jesus Christ be a spiritual physician, let us labour to hasten the cure of our souls. Consider,

(1) What a little time we have to stay here, and let that hasten the cure. Solomon saith, 'There is a time to be born, and a time to die' (Ecclesiastes 3:2), but mentions no time of living, as if that were so short that it were not worth the naming. The body is called a vessel (1 Thessalonians 4:4); this vessel is filled with breath, sickness broacheth it, and death draws it out. O hasten thy soul's cure, death is upon its swift march, and if that surprise you

suddenly, there is no cure to be wrought in the grave: 'There is no work, nor device, nor wisdom in the grave whither thou goest' (Ecclesiastes 9:10).

(2) Now is properly the time of healing, now is the day of grace, now Christ pours out his balsams, now he sends abroad his ministers and Spirit: 'Now is the accepted time' (2 Corinthians 6:2). There were certain healing days, wherein the king healed them that had the evil. The day of grace is a healing day: if we neglect the day of grace, the next day will be a day of wrath (Romans 2:5). O therefore hasten the cure of thy soul; rather neglect thy food than thy cure; sin will not only kill, but damn.

To get a cure, come to the healing pool of the sanctuary; the Spirit of God may on a sudden stir these waters; the next Sabbath, for ought thou knowest, may be a healing day to thy soul. Ask others to pray for you; when any disease is upon your body you desire the prayers of others; the prayers of the saints are precious balms and medicines to cure sick souls.

Is Jesus Christ a soul physician? Then let me speak to you who are in some measure healed of your damnable disease.

I have four things to say.

(1) *Break forth into thankfulness*. Though sin be not quite cured (there are still some grudgings of the disease), yet the reigning power of it is taken away; you are so healed that you shall not die (John 3:16; 11:26). Those that were cured by the brazen serpent afterwards died; but such as are healed by Christ, shall never die. Sin may molest, it shall not damn; O then what cause have you to admire and love your physician? The Lord Jesus hath taken out the core of your disease, and the curse. Publish your experiences: 'I will tell you what God hath done for my soul' (Psalm 116:16). As a man that hath been cured of an old disease, how glad and thankful is he? He will tell others of the medicine that cured him. So say, 'I will tell you what God hath done for my soul: he hath cured me of an old disease, a hard, unbelieving heart, a disease that hath sent millions to hell.' Truly

we may cheerfully bear any other sickness, if this soul-sickness be cured. Lord (saith Luther) strike and wound where thou wilt, if sin be pardoned. 'Let the high praises of God be in your mouth' (Psalm 149:6). God expects thankfulness as a tribute; he wonders men bring not their thank-offering: 'Were there not ten cleansed, but where are the nine?' (Luke 17:17).

(2) Are you healed? *Take heed of coming into infected company*, lest you take the infection; the wicked are devils to tempt to sin. Lot was the world's wonder that lived in Sodom when it was a pest-house, yet did not catch the disease.

(3) *Take heed of relapses*. Men are afraid of a relapse after they are cured; beware of soul relapses. Hath God softened thy heart? Take heed of hardening it. Hath he cured thee in some measure of deadness? Do not relapse into a drowsy security. Thou mayest have such an uproar and agony in thy conscience, as may make thee go weeping to thy grave. O take heed of falling sick again! 'Sin no more lest a worse thing come unto thee' (John 5:14).

(4) *Pity your friends that are sick unto death*; show your piety in your pity. Hast thou a child that is well and lusty, but hath a sick soul? Pity him, pray for him. David wept and fasted for his sick child (2 Samuel 12:16). Thy child hath the plague sore of the heart, and thou hast conveyed the plague to him; weep and fast for thy child. Hast thou a wife or a husband that though they do not keep their bed, yet the Lord knows they are sick, they are under the raging power of sin? O let thy bowels yearn over them! Lift up a prayer over them; the prayer of faith may save a sick soul. Prayer is the best physic that can be used in a desperate case; you that have felt the disease of sin, and the mercy of your physician, learn to pity others.

And lastly, Is Christ a soul physician? Then let us go to Christ to cure this sick, dying nation.

Britain, God knows, is a sick patient, 'The whole head is sick, the whole heart is faint.' The body politic hath a *cachexy*, it is ill all over: magistracy, ministry, commonality are diseased; and those who pretend to be our healers are physicians of no value. We have spent our money upon these physicians, but yet our sores are not healed: 'Why hast thou smitten us, and there is no healing for us?' (Jeremiah 14:19). Instead of healing us, those who should have been our physicians, have increased the nation's malady, by giving a toleration; this is like giving strong water in a fever, which doth more inflame the disease. Ah, sick Britain, because sinful Britain! Sick of error, uncleanness, drunkenness; so sick, that we may fear our funerals are approaching: and, which is the worst symptom, though balm hath been poured into our wounds, the precious ordinances of God have been applied, yet we are not healed; a sign of bad flesh that is so ill to be cured.

This sin-sickness in the land hath produced many direful effects; division, oppression, bloodshed, the very bowels and arteries of the nation are almost torn asunder, so that now God hath fulfilled that threatening upon us: 'I will make thee sick with smiting thee' (Micah 6:13). We had made ourselves sick with sinning, and God hath made us sick with smiting. Now what remains, but that we should go to the great physician, whose blood sprinkles many nations, that he should apply some healing medicines to dying Britain. God can with a word heal; he can give repentance as well as deliverance; he can put us in joint again. Let all the people of the land lie between the porch and the altar, saying, 'Spare thy people, O LORD' (Joel 2:17). Our prayers and tears may set Christ on work to heal us: 'Therefore he said that he would destroy them, had not Moses his servant stood in the breach to turn away his wrath' (Psalm 106:23). Let us never leave imploring our heavenly physician, till he lay a fig on England's boil, and cause it to recover.

9

The Beauty of Grace

'Grace unto you, and peace be multiplied'
(1 Peter 1:2).

The blessed apostle having felt the efficacy and sovereignty of grace, is taken up with the thoughts of it; and so sweet is this wine of paradise, that he commends it to those dispersed Christians to whom he writes, wishing them all increase. Grace unto you, and peace be multiplied.

The words run in the form of a salutation, 'grace unto you, and peace.' When we salute our friends, we cannot wish them a greater blessing than grace and peace: other mercies lie without the pale, and are dispersed in common to men; but grace is a special congiary and gift bestowed on them who are the favourites of heaven.

In the words observe first, the *connection*: Grace and peace. The way to have peace is to have grace; grace is the breeder of peace; the one is the root, the other the flower; peace is the sweet water that drops from the limbeck of a gracious heart. Secondly, the *order*: first grace, then peace. Grace hath the priority; grace and peace are two sisters, but grace is the eldest sister; and give me leave at this time to prefer the elder before the younger. 'Grace unto you be multiplied.'

For the illustration, we will consider: (1) What is meant by grace; (2) The Author of it; (3) Why it is called grace; (4) The cogency of it.

1. What is meant by grace
This word *grace* hath various meanings in Scripture.

1. Grace is sometimes taken for the favour of God: 'Noah found grace in the eyes of the LORD' (Genesis 6:8); God did cast a gracious aspect upon him.

2. Grace is taken for beauty; as we say such a thing is graceful, 'The flower falleth, and the grace of the fashion of it perisheth' (James 1:11).

3. Grace is taken figuratively, and improperly, for the show of grace; as we call that a face in a glass which is but the idea and resemblance of a face. So in John 2:23. 'Many believed in his name': that believing was but a show of faith, as Austin and Theophilact note.

4. Grace is taken in a genuine and proper sense; so in the text, 'Grace be multiplied'; it may admit of this description; grace is the infusion of a new and holy principle into the heart, whereby it is changed from what it was, and is made after God's own heart. Grace makes not only a civil, but a sacred change; it biasseth the soul heaven-ward, and stamps upon it the image and superscription of God.

2. The author of grace
He is the Spirit of God, who is therefore called the Spirit of grace (Zechariah 12:10). The Spirit is the fountain from whence crystal streams of grace flow. Man, as Clemens Alexandrinus observes, is God's harp or timbrel; the harp will not sound unless touched with the finger; so the heart of man cannot put forth any sweet melody or harmony, till first it be touched with the finger of God's Spirit. This blessed Spirit works grace in the subject both universally and progressively.

Universally
'The God of peace sanctify you wholly' (1 Thessalonians 5:23). The Spirit of God infuseth grace into all the faculties of the soul; though grace be wrought but in part, yet in every part; in the

understanding light, in the conscience tenderness, in the will consent, in the affections harmony; therefore grace is compared to heaven (Matthew 13:33), because it swells itself in the whole soul, and makes the conversation to swell and rise as high as heaven.

Progressively

The Spirit of God works grace progressively, he carries it on from one degree to another. Pelagians hold that the beginning of grace is from God; but the progress of grace is from ourselves; so God shall be the author of our faith, and we the finishers. God shall lay the first stone, and we the superstructure. But alas, there needs the continual influence of the Spirit to the carrying on the work of grace in our hearts. Should God withdraw his Spirit from the most holy men, their grace might fail and annihilate: if the sun withdraw its light, though ever so little, there follows darkness in the air; we need not only habitual grace, but assisting, exciting, subsequent grace. The ship needs not only the sails, but the winds to carry it; there needs not only the sails of our abilities and endeavours, but the wind of the Spirit to blow us to the heavenly port.

3. Why is the work of holiness in the heart called grace?

Because it hath a supereminency above nature; it is a flower which doth not grow in nature's garden; it is of a divine extraction (James 3:17). By reason we live the life of men, by grace we live the life of God.

It is called grace, because it is a work of free grace; every link in the golden chain of our salvation is wrought and enamelled with free-grace; that one should be sanctified, and not another, this is of grace; that God should pass by many of the noble, rich, learned, and graft his heavenly endowments on a more wild and luxuriant stock, a crabbed nature, weaker parts - well may it be called grace.

By why is not grace bestowed upon all?

We must hold with Zanchy, there is always a just reason of God's will; but in particular, I answer:

Firstly, God gives grace to one, and denies it to another to show his prerogative; God is not bound to give grace to all: 'I will have mercy on whom I will have mercy' (Romans 9:15). Suppose two malefactors are brought before the king, one he will pardon, but not the other; if any demand the reason, he will answer, it is my prerogative. So God will give grace to one, not to another; he will make one a vessel of mercy, the other a vessel of wrath, this is his prerogative. The apostle hath silenced all disputes of this kind: 'Who art thou that repliest against God? ... Hath not the potter power over the clay?' (Romans 9:20, 21). If we could suppose a plant to speak, why was not I made a bird, or a beast? Why should not I have reason? Just so it is when vain man enters into contest with God; why should not I have grace as well as another? Dispute not against prerogative; let not the clay syllogize with the potter.

Secondly, God may justly deny his grace to any wicked man, for two further reasons. The first is that man once had grace, and lost it; if a father gave his son a stock to trade with, and the son breaks, the father is not bound to set him up again. God gave Adam a stock of grace to begin the world with; Adam did break, and make all his children bankrupts; God is not tied to give him grace again. The second is that God may justly deny his grace to every wicked man, because he is a despiser of grace, he tramples this pearl under foot (Proverbs 1:7). Is God bound to give grace to them that despise it? If a king's pardon be rejected once, he is not bound to tender it any more; but I shall not launch forth any further into this.

4. The cogency and necessity of grace

It is most needful, because it fits us for communion with God: 'What communion hath light with darkness?' (2 Corinthians 6:14). God can no more converse with an ungracious soul, than a king can converse with a sow; it is by grace that we keep a constant intercourse with heaven.

Use 1. Exhort

Let me with the greatest zeal and earnestness persuade all who have souls to save, to endeavour after grace; grace will be desirable at death; it is as useful now, and more seasonable to look after: 'With all thy getting get understanding' (Proverbs 4:7). Alexander, being presented with a rich cabinet of King Darius, reserved it to put Homer's works in, as being of great value. The heart is a spiritual cabinet into which the jewel of grace should be put; we should desire grace above other things; above the gifts of the Spirit; nay above the comforts of the Spirit. Comfort is sweet, but grace is better than comfort; bread is better than honey. We may go to heaven without comfort, not without grace; it is grace that makes us blessed in life and death.

I shall show you twelve rare excellencies in grace. I shall set this fair virgin of grace before you, hoping that you will be tempted to fall in love with it.

1. *Grace hath a soul-quickening excellency in it*, 'The just shall live by faith' (Hebrews 10:38). Men void of grace are dead; they have breath, yet want life; they are walking ghosts (Ephesians 2:1). The life of sin is the death of the soul. A sinner hath all the signs of one that is dead; he hath no pulse; for the affections are the pulse of the soul; his pulse doth not beat after God. He hath no sense: 'Who being past feeling' (Ephesians 4:19). Dead things have no beauty, there is no beauty in a dead flower; dead things are not capable of privilege; the dead heir is not crowned. But grace is the vital artery of the soul; it doth not only irradiate, but animate; therefore it is called 'the light of life' (John 8:12). And believers are said to have their grave clothes pulled off, and to be alive from the dead (Romans 6:13). By grace the soul is grafted into Christ the true vine (John 15:5), and is made not only living but lively (1 Peter 1:3). Grace puts forth a divine energy into the soul.

2. *Grace hath a soul-enriching excellency*: 'Ye are enriched in all knowledge' (1 Corinthians 1:5). As the sun enricheth the world

with its golden beams, so doth knowledge bespangle and enrich the mind. Faith is an enriching grace: 'rich in faith' (James 2:5). Faith brings Christ's riches into the soul, it entitles to the promises. The promises are full of riches, justification, adoption, glory: faith is the key that unlocks this cabinet of the promises, and empties out their treasure into the soul. The riches of grace excel all other riches: 'The merchandise of it is better than the merchandise of silver' (Proverbs 3:14).

These riches make a man wise: wisdom is the best possession; other riches cannot make one wise. A man may have a full purse, and an empty brain. Many a rich heir, though he lives till he become of age, yet he never comes to years of discretion. But these riches of grace have power to make a man wise: 'The fear of the LORD is the beginning of wisdom' (Psalm 111:10). The saints are compared to wise virgins in Matthew 25:1-13. Grace makes a man wise to know Satan's devices and subtleties (2 Corinthians 2:11), it makes him wise unto salvation (2 Timothy 3:15). Grace gives the serpent's eye in the dove's head.

These spiritual riches sanctify other riches. Riches without grace are hurtful, they are golden snares; they are the bellows of pride, the fuel of lust; they set open hell gates for men; they are unblest blessings; but grace sanctifies our riches, it corrects the poison, it takes away the curse, it makes them beneficial to us; riches shall be certificates of God's love, wings to lift us up to paradise. Thus grace, by a divine chemistry, extracts heaven out of earth, and gives us not only venison but the blessing (Genesis 27).

Grace satisfies; other riches cannot (Ecclesiastes 5:10). Riches can no more fill the heart, than a triangle can fill a circle. But grace fills up every chink and hiatus of the soul; it dilates the heart, it ravisheth the affections with joy (Romans 15:13) - which joy, as Chrysostom saith, is a foretaste of heaven.

3. *Grace hath a soul-adorning excellency*, it puts a beauty and lustre upon a person: 'Whose adorning let it not be that outward adorning of plaiting the hair, and of wearing of gold, but let it be

the hidden man of the heart, even the ornament of a meek and quiet spirit, which is in the sight of God of great price; for after this manner in the old time, the holy women also who trusted in God adorned themselves' (1 Peter 3:3-5). If a man hath plate and jewels, cloth of gold, hangings of arras, these adorn the house, not the man; for the glory of a man is grace: 'She shall give to thine head an ornament of grace' (Proverbs 4:9). The graces are a chain of pearl that adorns Christ's bride; the heart inlaid and enamelled with grace, is like the 'King's daughter, all glorious within' (Psalm 45:13). A gracious soul is the image of God, curiously drawn with the pencil of the Holy Ghost; a heart beautified with grace is the angels' joy (Luke 15:7), and is God's lesser heaven (Isaiah 57:15; Ephesians 3:17). Reason doth not so far exceed sense, as grace doth reason; grace changeth corruption into perfection. Nothing so graceth a man as grace doth; grace is the purest complexion of the soul, for it makes it like God. Grace is the flower of delight which Christ loves to smell; grace is to the soul, as the eye to the body, as the sun to the world, as the diamond to the ring, it doth bespangle and beautify. A soul decked with grace is as the dove covered with silver wings and golden feathers.

4. *Grace hath a soul-cleansing excellency.* By nature we are defiled; sin is an impure issue, it is a befilthying thing (2 Corinthians 7:1). A sinner's heart is so black, that nothing but hell can pattern it; but grace is a spiritual laver; therefore it is called 'the washing of regeneration' (Titus 3:5). The grace of repentance cleanseth; Mary's tears, as they washed his feet, so they washed her heart; faith hath a cleansing virtue: 'Having purified their hearts by faith' (Acts 15:9).

Grace lays the soul a-whitening, it takes out the leopard spots, and turns the cypress into an azure beauty. Grace is of a celestial nature; though it doth not wholly remove sin, it doth subdue it; though it doth not keep sin out, it keeps it under; though sin in a gracious soul doth not die perfectly, yet it dies daily. Grace makes the heart a spiritual temple, which hath this inscription upon it, 'Holiness to the Lord'.

5. *Grace hath a soul-strengthening excellency*; it enables a man to do that which exceeds the power of nature. Grace teacheth us to mortify our sins, to love our enemies, to prefer the glory of Christ before our own lives. Thus the three children by the power of grace marched in the face of death; neither the sound of the music could allure them, nor the heat of the furnace affright them (Daniel 3:17). Grace is a Christian's armour of proof, which doth more than any other armour can; it not only defends him, but puts courage into him. Tertullian calls Athanasius an invincible adamant; grace makes us not only bear suffering, but glory in suffering (Romans 5:3). A soul steeled and animated with grace, can tread upon the lion and adder (Psalm 91:13), and with the leviathan, can laugh at the shaking of a spear (Job 41:29). Thus doth grace infuse an heroic spirit, and drive strength into a man, making him act above the sphere of nature.

6. *Grace hath a soul-raising excellency*; it is a divine sparkle that ascends; when the heart is divinely touched with the load-stone of the Spirit, it is drawn up to God. 'The way of life is above to the wise' (Proverbs 15:24): grace raiseth a man above others; he lives in the altitudes, while others creep on the earth, and are almost buried in it; a Christian by the wings of grace flies aloft; the saints 'mount up as eagles' (Isaiah 40:31). A believer is a citizen of heaven, there he trades by faith. Grace shoots the heart above the world (Psalm 139:17; Philippians 3:20). Grace gives us conformity to Christ, and communion with Christ: 'Our fellowship is with the Father, and with his Son Jesus Christ' (1 John 1:3). A man full of grace hath Christ in his heart, and the world under his feet; grace humbles, yet elevates.

7. *Grace hath a perfuming excellency*; it makes us a sweet odour to God. Hence grace is compared to those spices which are most

odoriferous and fragrant: 'Myrrh, cinnamon, frankincense' (Canticles 4:13). There is a double perfume that grace sends forth.

It perfumes our names: 'By faith the elders obtained a good report' (Hebrews 11:2). Grace was the spice which perfumed their names. How renowned was Abraham for his faith, Moses for his meekness, Phinehas for his zeal? What a fresh perfume do their names send forth to this day! The very wicked cannot but see a resplendent majesty in the graces of the saints; and though with their tongues they revile grace, yet with their hearts they reverence it. Thus grace is aromatical, it embalms the names of men; a gracious person when he dies, carries a good conscience with him, and leaves a good name behind him.

Grace perfumes our duties: 'Let my prayer be set forth before thee as incense' (Psalm 141:2). Noah's sacrifice was a perfume: the LORD smelled a sweet savour (Genesis 8:21). The sighs of a wicked man are an unsavoury breath, his solemn sacrifice is dung (Malachi 2:3). There is such a noisome stench comes from a sinner's duties, that God will not come near: 'I will not smell in your solemn assemblies' (Amos 5:21). Who can endure the smell of a dead corpse? But grace gives a fragrancy and redolency to our holy things: 'By faith Abel offered a more excellent sacrifice than Cain, God testifying of his gifts' (Hebrews 11:4). Abel's sacrifice was better scented, God smelled a sweet savour of it; for he testified of his gifts. If it be asked what this testimony was God gave of Abel's sacrifice? Hierom saith, God set his sacrifice on fire as in 1 Kings 18:38, so from heaven testifying his acceptance of Abel's offering. If grace doth so perfume you, wear this flower, not in your bosoms, but in your hearts.

8. *Grace hath a soul-ennobling excellency*, it doth ennoble a man: grace makes us vessels of honour, it sets us above princes and nobles. Theodosius thought it more dignity to be Christ's servant, and wear his livery laced with the silver graces of the Spirit, than to be great and renowned in the world. Sin doth debase a man, Christ tells wicked men their pedigree: 'Ye are of your

father the devil' (John 8:44): they may put the cloven foot in their scutcheon; an ungracious person is a vile person. In Nahum 1:14. God warns, 'I will make thy grave, for thou art vile': the Hebrew word for vile signifies to be lightly esteemed. There is nothing so vile but an ungracious man will do; he is ductile and facile to any thing, like wire, which will be bent awry; he will snare his conscience, stain his credit, run as a lackey after the sinful injunctions of men; but grace ennobles; he who is divinely inspired, as he is high born (1 John 3:1), so he acts suitably to his birth, he hates whatever is disingenuous and sordid. The saints are called kings and priests for their dignity (Revelation 1:6), and jewels for their value (Malachi 3:17).

9. *Grace hath a soul-securing excellency*, it brings safety along with it. You all desire to be safe in dangerous times; if sword or pestilence come, if death peep in at your windows, would you not be safe. Nothing will secure you in times of danger but grace; grace is the best life-guard; it sets Christians out of gunshot, and frees them from the power of hell and damnation: 'Righteousness delivers from death' (Proverbs 10:2). Do not righteous men die? Yes, but righteousness delivers from the sting of the first death, and the fear of the second. It was the saying of one, 'I am not afraid to die, but to be damned': but here is a believer's comfort, the fire of God's wrath can never kindle upon him. Grace is God's own image stamped on the soul, and he will not destroy his own image. Xerxes, the Persian, when he destroyed all the temples in Greece, caused the temple of Diana to be preserved for its beautiful structure. The soul which hath the beauty of holiness shining in it, shall be preserved for the glory of the structure; God will not suffer his own temple to be destroyed.

Would you be secured in evil times? Get grace and fortify this garrison; a good conscience is a Christian's fort-royal. David's enemies lay round about him; yet, saith he, 'I laid me down and slept' (Psalm 3:5). A good conscience can sleep in the mouth of a cannon. Grace is a Christian's coat of mail, which fears not the arrow or bullet. True grace may be shot at, but can never be shot through. Grace puts the soul into Christ, and there it is safe, as the bee in the hive, as the dove in the ark: 'There is no condemnation to them which are in Christ Jesus' (Romans 8:1).

10. *Grace hath a heart-establishing excellency.* 'It is a good thing that the heart be established with grace' (Hebrews 13:9). Before the infusion of grace, the heart is like a ship without a ballast; it wavers and tosseth, being ready to overturn; therefore a man void of grace is called a double-minded man (James 1:8). He acts for and against, as if he had two souls; he is unresolved, today of one mind, tomorrow of another; today he will hear a preacher that is orthodox, tomorrow one that is heterodox. He will be as the times are, and change his religion as fast as the chameleon doth his colour. Hearts unsanctified will be unsettled; they will face about to the rising side; they will follow not what is best, but what is safest. They are not for that religion which hath the Word to guide it, but for that which hath the sword to back it. This Seneca calls a mind that rolls up and down, and settles nowhere.

But grace doth consolidate and fix the heart: 'My heart is fixed, O God' (Psalm 57:7). Hypocrites are like meteors in the air; but David was a fixed star. Grace keeps the heart upright; and the more sincere, the more steadfast; grace carries the heart to God as the centre, and there it rests (Psalm 116:7). A gracious heart cleaves to God, and let whatever changes come, the soul is settled as a ship at anchor.

11. *Grace hath a preparatory excellency in it*; it prepares and fits for glory. Glory is the highest peg of our felicity, it transcends all our thoughts; glory can have no hyperbole. Now grace tunes and fits the soul for glory: 'Who hath called us to glory and virtue' (2 Peter 1:3). Virtue leads to glory. First you cleanse the vessel, and then pour in wine. God doth first cleanse us by his grace, and then pour in the wine of glory; the silver link of grace draws the golden link of glory after it: indeed grace differs little from glory; grace

is glory in the bud, and glory is grace in the flower. In short, glory is nothing else but grace commencing and taking its degrees.

12. *Grace hath an abiding excellency*; temporal things are for a season, but grace hath eternity stamped upon it, it is called durable riches (Proverbs 8:18). Other riches take wings and fly from us; grace takes wings and flies with us to heaven. Some tell us of falling away from grace. I grant seeming grace may be lost; a blazing comet will spend and evaporate; nay, saving grace may fail in the degree, it may suffer an eclipse, it may lose all its sweet fruit of joy and peace; but still there is sap in the vine, and 'the seed of God remains' (1 John 3:4). Grace is a blossom of eternity: 'The anointing that abides' (1 John 2:27). Colours laid in oil are durable; those hearts which are laid in oil, and have the anointing of God, hold their colours, and endure for ever: grace is compared to a 'river of the water of life' (John 7:38). This river can never be dried up, for the Spirit of God is the spring that feeds it. Grace is not like a lease which soon expires as the Pelagians would make it; today a believer, tomorrow an unbeliever; today justified, tomorrow unjustified; this would be like a lease soon run out. But God settles grace on the saints as an inheritance, and he will see that the entail shall never be cut off. He who hath true grace, can no more fall away than the angels, which are fixed stars in their heavenly orbs.

The arguments to prove the perpetuation of grace are:

(1) *God's election*; this I ground upon Romans 8:29, 30: 'Whom he did foreknow, he also did predestinate.' Predestination is the grand cause of the saints' preservation; God chooseth as well to salvation as to faith (2 Thessalonians 2:13). What shall make God's election void?

(2) *The power of God*: 'We are kept by the power of God through faith unto salvation' (1 Peter 1:5). I deny not but grace in itself may perish, (our grace is no better coin than Adam's) but grace in God's keeping cannot; the saints' graces of themselves

may break as glasses, but these glasses in the hand of God never break.

(3) *God's solemn engagement*; the Lord hath passed it under hand and seal; he hath given bond for the saints' perseverance: 'I will make an everlasting covenant with them, that I will not turn away from them, and they shall not depart from me' (Jeremiah 32:40). A believer's charter is confirmed under the broad seal of heaven; and if grace doth not endure to eternity, it is either because God wants power to make good what he hath decreed, or truth to make good what he hath promised; either of which to assert were blasphemy.

Besides all this, Jesus Christ our blessed high priest, who hath the golden plate on his forehead, appears in the court; and as he poured out blood on the cross, so he pours forth prayers in heaven for the saints' perseverance: 'he ever liveth to make intercession for them' (Hebrews 7:25). And Christ is not only a priest, but a Son; therefore likely to prevail; which puts the matter out of doubt, what Christ prays for as he is man, he hath power to give as he is God: 'Father, I will' (John 17:24): 'Father,' there he prays as man; 'I will,' there he gives as God.

So grace is an abiding thing. Christians, you may lose your friends, your estates, your lives, but you shall never lose your grace. Those who hold falling away from grace would make a believer wear Cain's mark, which was a continual shaking and trembling in his flesh; they would spill a Christian's cordial, and break a link of the chain of salvation.

Use 2. Trial

Let us try whether our grace be true; there is something looks like grace which is not. Chrysostom saith the devil hath a counterfeit claim to all the graces, and he would deceive us with it. Lapidaries have ways to try their precious stones; let us try our grace by a Scripture touchstone: the painted Christian shall have a painted paradise.

(1) The truth of grace is seen by a displacency and antipathy

against sin: 'I hate every false way' (Psalm 119:104): grace sets itself against complexion sins (Psalm 18:23), and against the sins of the times (Revelation 2:2).

(2) Grace is known by the growth of it, growth evidenceth life. Dead things grow not; a picture will not grow; a hypocrite, who is but a picture of religion, doth not grow; a good Christian grows in love to Christ, in humility, in good works: 'He shall grow as the lily, his branches shall spread, and his beauty shall be as the olive tree, and his smell as Lebanon' (Hosea 14:5,6). When the Spirit of God distils as dew upon the soul, it makes grace flourish, and put forth into maturity.

(3) True grace will make us willing to suffer for Christ. Grace is like gold, it will abide the 'fiery trial' (1 Peter 1:7). And if upon a serious scrutiny and trial we find that we have the right jewel, 'the grace of God in truth' (Colossians 1:6), this will be a deathbed cordial; we may with Simeon, 'depart in peace', being assured that though we cannot resist death, yet we shall overcome it.

Use 3. Direction
Let me lay down some directions for the attaining of grace.

Firstly, if we would be enriched with this jewel of grace, let us take pains for it; we are bid to make a hue and cry after knowledge, and to search for it, as a man that searcheth for a vein of gold (Proverbs 2:2, 3). Our salvation cost Christ blood, it will cost us sweat.

Secondly, let us go to God for grace; he is called 'the God of all grace' (1 Peter 5:10). We could lose grace of ourselves, but we cannot find it of ourselves. The sheep can wander from the fold, but cannot return without the help of the shepherd; go to the God of all grace; God is the first planter, the promoter, the perfecter of grace. God is the Father of lights (James 1:17). He must light up this candle of grace in the soul; grace is in his gift; it is not an impropriation, but a donative.

O then go to God in prayer, lay thy heart before him and say, Lord, I want grace; I want an humble, believing heart, and thou art the God of all grace, all my springs are in thee. O enrich me with grace, deny me not this before I die. What is gold in the bag, if I have no oil in the lamp? Give me 'that anointing of God.' I read in thy word of 'the fruits of the Spirit'. Lord, my heart is a barren soil, plant some of these supernatural fruits in me, that I may be more useful and serviceable. Lord, I cannot be put off with other things. Who wilt thou give grace to, if not to such as ask, and are resolved not to give over asking?

Thirdly, if you would have grace, engage the prayers of others in your behalf. He is like to be rich, who hath several stocks going; he is in the way of spiritual thriving, who hath several stocks of prayer going for him. If you had a child that were sick, you would beg the prayers of others. Thou hast a soul that is sick, sick of pride, lust, 'sick unto death'. O beg the prayers of godly friends, that God will heal thee with his grace. A Moses and Jacob have much power with God: believers can prevail sometimes not only for themselves, but for their friends (James 5:16). A godly man's prayers may do you more good than if he should bestow upon you all his lands of inheritance.

Fourthly, if you would have grace, frequent the means of grace, lie at the pool of Bethesda, wait at the posts of wisdom's door. Inward grace is wrought by outward means; the preaching of the Word is God's engine that he uses for working grace; it is called 'the rod of his strength' (Psalm 110:2), and 'the breath of his lips' (Isaiah 11:4). By this he causes breath to enter; out of this golden pipe of the sanctuary, God empties the golden oil of grace into the soul; the ministry of the gospel is called 'the ministry of the Spirit' in 2 Corinthians 3:8, because the Spirit of God ordinarily makes use of this to work grace; this ministry of the Spirit is to be preferred before the ministry of angels.

Why is the word preached the ordinary means to convey grace? Why not conference or reading?

The reason is, because God hath appointed it to this end, and he will grace his own ordinances: 'it pleased God' (1 Corinthians 1:21). What reason could be given why the waters of Damascus should not have as sovereign virtue to heal Naaman's leprosy as the waters of Jordan? Only this, because the Lord did appoint and sanctify the one to this work, and not the other. If therefore we would have grace, let us wait where the manna falls, and there expect the dew of the Spirit to fall with the manna; the power of God goes along with his Word.

How should we delight in ordinances! Sleidan saith there was a church in France formerly, which the Protestants called Paradise; as if they thought themselves in paradise while they were in the house of God; those ordinances should be our paradise which are 'the power of God to salvation.'

10

The Trees of Righteousness Blossoming, and Bringing Forth Fruit

'Being filled with the fruits of righteousness which are
by Jesus Christ, unto the glory and praise of God'
(Philippians 1:11).

The blessed apostle in this chapter makes a solemn prayer to God for these Philippians; and amongst the rest, he puts up two rare petitions for them. First, that they might be sincere (verse 10); and second, that they might be fruitful, in the words of the text, 'Being filled with the fruits of righteousness'. Where is observable: (1) The matter, 'Being filled with fruits'; (2) The manner of production, 'by Jesus Christ'; (3) The end, 'which are to the glory and praise of God.'

The doctrine taken from this verse is 'that Christians should above all things endeavour after fruitfulness.' The saints are called 'trees of righteousness' (Isaiah 61:3). These rational trees must not only bring forth leaves, but fruit; 'Being filled with the fruits of righteousness.' For the further amplifying of this, there are two things to be inquired into: (1) How a Christian brings forth fruit; (2) What is the fruit he brings forth.

1. How a Christian brings forth fruit

He brings forth fruit 'in the vine'; by nature we are barren; there is not one good blossom growing on us; but when by faith we are ingrafted into Christ, then we grow and fructify: 'As the branch cannot bear fruit of itself, except it abide in the vine, no more can ye except ye abide in me' (John 15:4). Jesus Christ is that blessed root which shoots up that sap of grace into his branches. The Pelagians tell us we have sufficiency of ourselves to bring forth good fruit: but how improper is this? Doth not the root contribute to the branches? Is it not of Christ's precious fullness that we receive? (John 1:16). Therefore it is observable Christ calls the spouse's grace his grace: 'I have gathered my myrrh with my spice' (Canticles 5:1). Christ saith not, thy myrrh, but my myrrh. If the saints bear any spiritual fruit, they are beholden to Christ for it, it is his myrrh: 'From me is thy fruit found' (Hosea 14:8).

2. What that fruit is which a good Christian brings forth.

1. A Christian brings forth *inward* fruit: 'Love, joy, peace, long-suffering, gentleness, goodness, faith' (Galatians 5:22). Thus fruit is sweet and mellow, growing under the Sun of righteousness; this is that ripe fruit God delights to taste of (Micah 7:1).

2. A Christian brings forth *outward* fruit.

The fruit of good discourse: 'A wholesome tongue is a tree of life' (Proverbs 15:4). Gracious speeches fall from the lips of a godly man, as fruit from a tree.

The fruit of good works (Colossians 1:10). God will say at the last day, show me thy faith by thy works (James 2:18). A true saint doth all the good he can, 'honouring the Lord with his substance'; he knows he is to be in the world but a while, therefore lives much in a little time, and crowds up a great deal of work in a little room; it was Christ's speech not long before his suffering, 'I have finished the work which thou gavest me to do' (John 17:4). How can they be said to finish their work, that never yet began a good work?

3. A Christian brings forth *kindly* fruit.

The godly man bringeth forth his fruit (Psalm 1:3), that is, he brings forth that fruit which is proper for him to bear. But what is this kindly and proper fruit? I answer, when we are good in our callings and relations: in a magistrate, justice is kindly fruit

(Deuteronomy 16:19), in a minister, zeal (Acts 17:16), in a parent, instruction (Deuteronomy 4:10), in a child, reverence (Ephesians 6:1), in a master, good example (Genesis 18:19, Ephesians 6:9), in a servant, obedience (1 Peter 2:18), in a husband, love (Ephesians 5:25), in a wife, submission (Ephesians 5:22), in a tradesman, diligence (Exodus 20:9), in a soldier, innocence (Luke 3:14). A tree of God's planting brings forth his fruit, that which is suitable and proper.

I shall never believe him to be good, that doth not bear kindly fruit. A good Christian but a bad master, a good Christian but a bad parent, doth not sound well. That minister can no more be good which wants zeal, than that wine is good which wants spirits. That magistrate can no more be good which wants justice, than that pillar is good which is not upright. That child can no more be good who doth not honour his parent, than a traitor can be said to be loyal. When Absalom did rise up in rebellion against his father, the mule which he rode upon (as if she were weary of carrying such a burden) resigns up her load to the great thick oak, and there left him hanging by the head betwixt heaven and earth, as neither fit to ascend the one, nor worthy to tread upon the other.

Let Christians be persuaded to bring forth proper and genuine fruit, and shine forth in their relations: consider:

He who is not good in his relations goes under the just suspicion of an *hypocrite*. Let a man seem to be a penitent, or zealot, yet if he bear not fruit proper to his station, he is no tree of righteousness, but some wild degenerate plant. There are some who will pray, hear sermons, discourse well; this is good: but 'what means the bleating of the sheep'? They are not good in their relations; this discovers they are foundered and unsound. A good Christian labours to fill his relations, and to go through all the parts of religion, as the sun through all the signs of the zodiac. I like not those Christians, who, though they seem to be travelling to heaven, yet leave the duties of their relations as a *terra incognita*, which they never come near.

The excellency of a Christian is to bring forth *proper* fruit.

Wherein lies the goodness of a member in the body, but to discharge its proper office? The eye is to see, the ear to hear, etc. So the excellency of a Christian is to bring forth that fruit which God hath assigned to him. What is a thing good for which doth not do its proper work? What is a clock good for that will not strike? What is a ship good for that will not sail? What is a rose good for that doth not smell? What is that professor good for that doth not send forth a sweet perfume in his relation? The commendation of a thing is when it puts forth its proper virtue.

Not to bring forth suitable fruit *spoils* all the other fruit which we bring forth. If a man were to make a medicine, and should leave out the chief ingredient, the medicine would lose its virtue. If one were to draw a picture, and should leave out an eye, it would spoil the picture. There are many to whom Christ will say at the day of judgment as to the young man in Luke 18:22, 'Yet lackest thou one thing.' Thou hast prayed, and fasted, and heard sermons, 'yet lackest thou one thing', thou hast not been good in thy relations.

Relative graces do much *beautify* and set off a Christian: it is the beauty of a star to shine in its proper orb; relative grace doth bespangle a Christian.

4. A good Christian brings forth *seasonable* fruit.
He bringeth forth fruit in his season, (Psalm 1:3); everything is beautiful in his time (Ecclesiastes 3:11) That may be good at one time, which at another may be out of season. There is a great deal of skill in the right timing of a thing; duties of religion must be performed in the fit juncture of time.

1. Christian duties that relate to our neighbour must be observed in their season.
(1) *Our reproving others must be seasonable.* Reproof is a duty; when we see others walk irregularly, like soldiers that march out of rank and file, we ought mildly, yet gravely, to tell them of their sin (Leviticus 19:17). But let this fruit be brought forth in its season.

Do it privately: 'Go and tell him his faults between him and thee alone' (Matthew 18:15).

Do it when thou seest him in the best temper, not when his passions are up; that were pouring oil on the flame; but when his spirit is meekened and calmed. You put the seal on the wax when it is soft and pliable; there is a time when men's spirits are more flexible and yielding; that is the fittest time to stamp a reproof upon them, and it is likeliest to take impression. When Abigail reproved Nabal, it was in the right season; not when he was in wine, but when he was in his wits, and was fit to hear a reproof (1 Samuel 25:37).

Another season for reproof is in the time of affliction. Affliction tames men's spirits and now a word of reproof spoken prudentially may work with the affliction: a bitter potion is not refused if in case of extremity of pain. Affliction opens the ear to discipline.

(2) *Our comforting of others must be seasonable*: 'A word spoken in due season, how good is it?' (Proverbs 15:23). When we see one fallen into sin, and with Peter weeping bitterly, O now a word of comfort will do well. The incestuous Corinthian being deeply humbled, the apostle calls for oil and wine to be poured into his wounds. 'Ye ought rather to comfort him', and the reason is given, 'lest perhaps such an one should be swallowed up of sorrow' (2 Corinthians 2:7). When the soul is wounded for sin, now bring the mollifying ointment of a promise. Hang out free grace's colours, display the glory of God's attributes, his mercy and truth to the sinner. When the spirit is broken, a word of comfort spoken in season is the putting it in joint again. This is to bring forth seasonable fruit, when we give wine to them that are of a heavy heart; 'pleasant words are as an honeycomb, sweet to the soul.' Job's friends pretended to comfort him, but instead of pouring oil into the wound, they poured in vinegar.

2. Duties of religion that relate to God must be performed in their season.

(1) *Mourning for sin is a duty*; God loves a contrite heart (Psalm 51:17). How powerful with God is the weeping rhetoric that a poor sinner uses! But yet there is a time when weeping may not be so seasonable. When God hath given us some eminent signal deliverance, and this mercy calls aloud to us to rejoice, but we hang our harps on the willows and sit weeping; this sadness is fruit out of season.

There was a special time at the feast of tabernacles, when God called his people to rejoicing; 'Seven days shalt thou keep a solemn feast unto the Lord thy God, and thou shalt surely rejoice.' Now if the Israelites had sat heavy and disconsolate at that time when God called them to rejoicing, it had been very unseasonable, like mourning at a wedding. When we are called to thanksgiving, and we mingle our drink with tears, is not this to be highly unthankful for mercy? God would have his people humble, but not ungrateful. It is the devil's policy either to keep us from duty, or else to put us upon it when it is least in season.

(2) *Rejoicing is a duty* (Psalm 33:1). But when God by some special providence calls us to weeping, now joy is unseasonable; this is that which God complains of in Isaiah 22:12,13: 'In that day did the LORD of hosts call to weeping, and behold joy and gladness,' etc. Oecolampadius and others think it was in the time of King Ahaz, when the signs of God's anger, like a blazing star, did appear. Then to be given to mirth was very unseasonable: 'Surely this iniquity shall not be purged from you till ye die, saith the LORD God of hosts' (verse 14). This is a concise form of an oath, as if God had said, I swear it shall not by any prayer or sacrifice be expiated; the fruit of joy must be brought forth in its season.

To read at home, when the word is a-preaching, or the sacrament celebrating, is unseasonable, nay sinful, as Hushai said in 2 Samuel 17:7: 'The counsel is not good at this time'. One duty is to prepare for another, but not to jostle out another; fruit must put forth seasonably. The great God who hath appointed the duties of his worship hath appointed also the time. If, when public ordinances are administered, any person, whether out of pride or sloth, shall stay at home, though he may have his private devotions, yet he brings forth fruit out of season. Let that man know he shall bear his sin.

Let all the trees of righteousness bring forth seasonable fruit; in prosperity be thankful, in adversity patient. 'To every thing there is a season' (Ecclesiastes 3:1). The Psalmist saith, 'He appointed the moon for seasons' (Psalm 104:19).

To excite to seasonable fruit, consider:

1. The seasonableness of a thing puts a value and preciousness upon it. Duties of religion performed in their season are glorious.

2. Creatures, by the instinct of nature, observe their season: 'Yea the stork in the heaven knoweth her appointed times ...' (Jeremiah 8:7). And shall not Christians observe their seasons, when to mourn, when to rejoice?

3. Duties of religion not well timed are dangerous: mourning in a time of joy, private duties in time of public, is unseasonable, and will prove prejudicial.

Use 1. Inform

It shows us who is a Christian in God's calendar, namely, the fruit-bearing Christian. As soon as the sap of grace is infused, it puts forth itself in evangelical fruit. No sooner was Paul converted, but he became a plant of renown, he did bring forth rare fruit, humility, faith, heavenly-mindedness; he was one of the most fruitful trees that ever God planted in his vineyard. The Philippian jailer, when God had changed him from a wild tree to a tree of righteousness, brought forth sweet and generous fruit. How kindly did he use the apostles? He set meat before them, and washed their wounds. He who was before their jailer becomes now their nurse and physician.

Use 2. Reproof
Here is an indictment against three sorts.

Such as bring forth no fruit
'Israel is an empty vine' (Hosea 10:1). O how many unfruitful hearers are there, who evaporate into nothing but froth and fume, being like those ears which run out all into straw! They give God neither the early fruit nor the latter. There are many Christians like arbours, covered only with the leaves of profession; they may be compared to the wood of the vine, which is good for nothing (Ezekiel 15:2-5). He who hath not the fruits of the Spirit, hath not the Spirit, and 'he who hath not the Spirit is none of Christ's' (Romans 8:9). And if he be not Christ's, whose is he then? I fear the sin of this age is unfruitfulness. Never more labouring in God's vineyard, and yet never less fruit; instead of the fig-tree and the pomegranate, we have abundance of barren willows growing among us. Ministers say they fear they 'spend their labour in vain'; many are perverted, few converted.

To the unfruitful Christian let me say four things.

Firstly, unfruitfulness is a shame: barrenness of old was counted a great shame. For a tree in winter to be unfruitful is no great wonder; but in the spring and summer, to be without fruit is a reproach to the tree. So, in the winter of ignorance and popery to have less fruit was less culpable; but in the spring-time of the gospel, when the Sun of Righteousness hath shined so gloriously in our horizon, to be without fruit is a reproach not to be wiped away.

Secondly, what account can the unfruitful Christian give to God? God will come with this question, Where is your fruit? A godly man dies full of fruit: 'Thou shalt come to thy grave in full age, like as a shock of corn ...' (Job 5:26). The unfruitful Christian comes to his grave, not as a shock of corn, but as a bundle of straw, fit only for the fire. It is good to bethink ourselves what answer we shall give to God for our barrenness. The Lord hath planted us in a rich soil; he may say to us as to his vineyard in Isaiah 5:1

ff. 'My beloved hath a vineyard in a very fruitful hill, and he fenced it, and planted it with the choicest vine ... and he looked that it should bring forth grapes, and it brought forth wild grapes'.

Hilly places are judged the fittest for vines to grow in (Psalm 80:10). There the sun comes best, and is of more force for ripening the grapes. In a fruitful hill, there is very fat, rich soil. So may God say to us, I have planted you in a hilly place, you have been higher than the nations round about you, you have even been lifted up to heaven with ordinances. The sunbeams of mercy, and Sion's silver drops, have fallen upon you. But where is your fruit? Your enjoyments are great, but what are your improvements? Whom God finds without fruit, he leaves without excuse.

Thirdly, they that do not bring forth good fruit shall never taste of the fruits that grow in heaven. Heaven is the garden of God, the paradise of pleasure, where the most rare delicious fruits grow; there are fruits that the angels themselves delight to feed on. If you do not bring God your fruit, you shall never taste his fruit: you that do not bring forth the fruits of righteousness shall never taste the fruits of paradise. O present Christ with your sweet spices, give him your myrrh, your spiced wine. Your myrrh, that is, repentance; this, though it be bitter to you, is sweet to Christ. Those who have no myrrh or wine to give to God, shall never feed upon the Tree of Life, which bears several sorts of fruit.

Fourthly, think of the heavy doom which will be passed upon the unfruitful person: 'Cast ye the unprofitable servant into outer darkness' (Matthew 25:30). This man had not embezzled his talent, but because he did not trade with it, and bring forth fruit, he is therefore sentenced.

It reproves such as bring forth evil fruit.
They are not the trees of the garden, but the wilderness; their hearts are a fruitful soil for sin, they bring forth pride, malice, superstition, etc.

It reproves such as bring forth good fruit, but to a bad end.
'Israel is an empty vine, he bringeth forth fruit unto himself'
(Hosea 10:1): a man had as good bring forth no fruit, as bring
forth fruit unto himself.

What is it for one to bring forth fruit unto himself?

When all the good he doth is for the magnifying of himself;
the worm of pride gets into his fruit and spoils it. Prayer is good;
but when a man prays only to show his parts, this is to bring forth
fruit unto himself. Some pride it in their humbling confessions,
which is as if Benhadad's servants had been proud when they
came before the king with ropes upon their heads (1 Kings
20:31). Works of mercy are good, but when a man gives alms, not
so much to feed the poor, as to feed his pride, now he brings forth
fruit to himself, and this fruit is worm-eaten. God will say to all
such self-seekers, as once he did to the people of the Jews: 'When
ye fasted and mourned, did ye at all fast unto me, even to me?'
(Zechariah 7:5). Sinners, did ye not bring forth fruit unto
yourselves?

Use 3. Exhort
Let this exhort all to fruitfulness.
How happy were it, if it might be said of us as of Joseph in
Genesis 49:22, 'Joseph is a fruitful bough'? We love to see every
thing fruitful. If there be a tree in our orchard, though with ever
such fair leaves, we value it not unless there be fruit. When you
come into your garden, you complain if you see no fruit; such a
root is set, but it doth not grow. We love to see fruitfulness
everywhere, and why not in our hearts? O let the precious grapes
and figs we bear evidence that we are trees of God's planting. We
often plant trees to be a shade to the house; God cares for no such
trees as are only for shade, he loves fruit. Arabia is called Felix,
because of the sweet fruits which grow there, frankincense, with
other perfumes and spices. That Christian may be entitled Felix,
happy, that hath the sweet fruits of the Spirit growing in his heart.
Be fruit-bearing trees! This is the emblem of a good Christian, he

is never without fruit, either blooming in his affections, or fructifying in his conversation.

That I may persuade Christians to fruitfulness, I desire them to weigh these five things.

Firstly, fruit is that which God *expects* from us, we are his plantations; and, 'Who planteth a vineyard, and eateth not of the fruit thereof?' (1 Corinthians 9:7). Let us not be as Pharaoh's kine, which devoured the fat, and yet still were lean; let us not be still devouring sermons, yet never the fatter.

Secondly, fruitfulness is one of the most distinctive characters of a Christian: 'The root of the righteous yieldeth fruit' (Proverbs 12:12). Fruitfulness differeth a saint from a hypocrite! The hypocrite is all for show and pretence, he hath fair leaves, but the 'root of the righteous yieldeth fruit'. Fruit can no more be separated from faith, than moisture from the air. It is the very definition of a branch in Christ that 'it bears fruit' (John 15:2). As a man differs from a beast by reason, a beast differs from a plant by sense, a plant differs from a stone by vegetation, so a good Christian differs from a hypocrite by fruit. Fruitfulness puts a difference between the sound tree and the hollow tree.

But may not hypocrites bring forth fruit?

Hypocrites do not bring forth fruit in the Vine; they bring forth in the strength of parts, not in the strength of Christ. They bring forth something like fruit, but it is not the right fruit. The fruit they bear is *not sweet*. The crab may bear fruit as well as the pearmain; but this excels in sweetness. The hypocrite may pray and give alms as well as a child of God, but there is a difference in the fruit; the fruit of the regenerate is mellow, it is sweetened with faith, it is ripened with love. The hypocrite's fruit is sour and harsh; he doth not bring forth pomegranates, but crabs, not figs, but wild grapes. This seeming fruit of hypocrites *dies and comes to nothing*: 'He is cast forth as a branch, and is withered' (John 15:6). The hypocrite's fruit is like the grass upon the house tops, which withereth before it groweth up (Psalm 129:6; Matthew 13:6).

Thirdly, fruitfulness *adorns* a Christian as the fruit adorns the tree. A fruit-bearing Christian is an ornament to religion; the more fruitful the branch is, the more fair to look on. A dead tree, as it is unserviceable, so it is uncomely. A Christian decked with the fruits of righteousness is beautiful and glorious.

Fourthly, fruitfulness is a *good evidence to show for heaven*; the fruits of love, humility, good works, are (as Bernard saith) seeds of hope, signs of predestination, the happy presages of future glory. The righteousness of faith is always accompanied with the fruits of righteousness. He that can show good fruit, goes full sail to heaven.

Fifthly, God *delights* in his fruitful trees; when his garden flourisheth he will walk there; he who curseth the barren tree, will taste of the fruitful tree: 'I am come into my garden, my sister, my spouse: I have gathered my myrrh with my spice' (Canticles 5:1).

It exhorts them that do bear fruit, that they would bring forth more fruit.

Do not think you have fruit enough, but bring forth further degrees of sanctity. 'Every branch that beareth fruit, he purgeth it that it may bring forth more fruit' (John 15:2). Grace is like the morning light which increaseth more and more to the full meridian of glory. Christians should be like that ground in the parable which brought forth 'some sixty, some an hundred fold' (Matthew 13:8). He who hath a little gold labours to increase it; and is not grace more precious than gold? Some Christians have a little fruit, and they think that is well; like trees that have an apple or two growing upon them to show that they are of the right kind: 'Two or three berries in the top of the uppermost bough' (Isaiah 17:6). They are like the church at Philadelphia which had 'a little strength' (Revelation 3:8), so they have a little faith, a spark of love. Christ chides a little faith (Matthew 14:31). Christians should increase with the increase of God (Colossians 2:19). Christ compares the breasts of the spouse to clusters of grapes for fruitfulness (Canticles 7:7). O labour to be Christians of degrees; the apostle prays for the Philippians that their love might abound 'yet more and more' (Philippians 1:9).

Now that I may press Christians who have fruit to bring forth more fruits of patience, humility, love, etc., consider:

(1) This is the end why we have new cost laid out upon us, that we should bring forth more fruit. The Lord is still manuring us; not a week, not a day, but he is at new cost with us, he rains down golden showers. And why is God at this charge with us, but that we may bring forth more fruit?

(2) The fuller we are of fruit, the more we are like Christ, who was 'full of grace and truth' (John 1:14). He received the Spirit 'without measure' (John 3:34). This tree of life was ever bearing; and he brought forth several sorts of fruit, wisdom, righteousness, sanctification, etc. The more we are filled with the fruits of righteousness, the more we resemble the Sun of Righteousness. We were elected to this end, to be made like Christ (Romans 8:29). Then are we most like this blessed Vine when we bear full clusters.

(3) The more fruit a Christian brings forth, the more will Christ love him. 'Now, saith Leah, will my husband be joined unto me, because I have born him three sons' (Genesis 29:34). When we bear much fruit, then will Christ's heart be joined to us. Christ will pardon a weak faith, he will honour a great faith. It was not a sparkle of faith Christ commended in Mary Magdalene, but love flaming: 'she loved much' (Luke 7:74). Christians, would you be like that beloved disciple which 'leaned on the bosom of Jesus'? Would you have much love from Christ? Let him have much fruit from you.

(4) Bearing much fruit will usher in abundance of comfort into the soul in these two exigencies. Firstly, *in the hour of tentation.* Satan will be sure to besiege the weakest Christian; all his darts fly that way, and a strong tentation may overcome a weak faith. But a flourishing faith stands like a cedar, and is not blown down by the wind of tentation. A strong faith can stop the mouth of the devil, that roaring lion (1 Peter 5:9).

Secondly, store of fruit will give comfort in the hour of death; a little grace will make us above the fear of death. O what joy will it be on the deathbed, when a Christian can bring his sheaves full of corn! When he can show his five talents that he hath gained by trading! When there is not only a drop or two of oil, but his lamp full of oil! What though the devil show God our debts, if we can show him our fruit. O how sweet will death be! It will not be a destruction, but a deliverance. Death, like a whirlwind, may blow down the tree of the body, but it cannot blast the fruit of our graces. The trees of righteousness carry their fruit with them: 'their works follow them' (Revelation 14:13). The Christian who abounds in holiness may say with Simeon in Luke 2:29, 'Lord, now lettest thou they servant depart in peace.' He who bears but a little fruit departs in safety; but he who bears much fruit departs in peace.

(5) Consider what need we have to be putting forth still more fruit; our graces are yet in their nonage. Indeed in heaven this doctrine will be out of season, we shall not need to hear it; then we shall have done growing, being arrived at our full stature; then our light shall be clear, and our love perfect. But while we live here, there is something 'lacking in our faith' (1 Thessalonians 3:10). Therefore we had need increase the stock of grace, and bring forth more fruit. Our grace is eclipsed with sin, our faith is full of unbelief; now as when the sun is eclipsed, it is by degrees getting out of the eclipse, and it shines brighter and brighter till it recovers its perfect lustre; so it must be with us, we must be getting out of the eclipse till we shall arrive at our perfect lustre in glory.

(6) He who doth not increase to more fruitfulness will soon be on the losing hand; he that hath not more faith will quickly have less: 'Thou hast left thy first love.' It is with grace as it is with fire; if it be not blown up and increased, it will soon decay. Such as thrive not in their spiritual estate, we may perceive sadly to decline. Though a Christian cannot lose the seed of grace, yet he may lose the actings of grace, and the comfort of grace. Therefore

bring forth more fruit: no sooner doth a Christian begin to stand still, but you may perceive him going backward.

(7) The more your fruit is increased, the more your glory is increased; he whose pound gained ten, was made ruler over ten cities. If you would have your crown hung full of jewels, let your boughs be hung full of fruit.

Use 4. Direction
I shall lay down some means to fruitfulness.

(1) Be *sensible* of unfruitfulness. Many might have been fruitful in grace, if they had not conceited themselves so; he that thinks himself fruitful enough is barren enough; be sensible of your wants; it is better to complain than presume.

(2) If you would be fruitful, *remove* those things which will hinder fruitfulness. First, avoid cherishing any secret lust in the heart; sin lived in, is like vermin to the tree, which destroys the fruit; grace cannot thrive in a sinful heart. Secondly, watch the love of riches: 'The cares of the world choked the seed' (Matthew 13:22). The love of sin poisons the fruit, the love of riches chokes it.

(3) The third means to fruitfulness is *weeping for sin*. Moisture helps germination in trees; holy tears do water the trees of God, and make them more fruitful. Mary Magdalene, a weeping plant, how fruitful was she in love to Christ? Moist grounds, as your marshes, are most fertile. The soul that is moistened and steeped in tears is most frugiferous: never did David's graces flourish more, than when he watered his couch with tears.

(4) If you would be fruitful, often apply the blood of Christ, and the promises.

Apply the blood of Christ. Naturalists say, that blood applied to the root of some trees makes them bear better. Sure I am, the blood of Christ applied to the heart makes it flourish more in holiness. None so fruitful as a believer; 'I know,' saith St Paul, 'whom I have believed'; there was the applying blood to the root of the tree, and how fruitful was he in zeal and love to Christ, heroical courage! He that believes Christ died for him never thinks he can do or suffer enough for Christ. When we read and pray, we do but water the branches; when we believe, we water the root of the tree and make it fruitful.

Apply the promises. Husbandmen have an art to comfort the spirits of the root to make the tree bear better. Apply the promises; these are for comforting the spirits of a Christian, and then he puts forth fruit more vigorously. It is an experiment in nature, the root of the pine tree watered with wine doth cause it to flourish. The promises are as wine to water the trees of righteousness, whereby they spread and augment more in grace. Ever preserve the spirits of the tree if you would have it bear. A pensive, dejected soul is less fruitful; but when through the promises, a Christian's heart is cheered and comforted, he is enriched with pleasant fruits; he is like a tree laden with fruit.

(5) Another means to fruitfulness is *humility.* The low grounds are most fruitful: 'The valleys are covered with corn' (Psalm 65:13). The humble heart is the fruitful heart. The largest and fairest fruits of the Spirit grow in a lowly Christian: 'God gives grace to the humble' (1 Peter 5:5). Saint Paul calls himself the least of saints, yet he was the chief of the apostles. The Virgin Mary was low in her own eyes, but this lowly plant did bear that blessed Vine which brought the fruit of salvation into the world.

(6) If you would be fruitful in grace, *be much in good conference*; 'Then they that feared the LORD spake often one to another' (Malachi 3:16). There is an observation some have concerning the sympathy of plants; some plants will bear better near other trees than when they grow alone, as is seen in the myrtle and olive. This holds true in divinity; the trees of righteousness, when they associate and grow near together thrive best in godliness. The communion of saints is an excellent means for fruitfulness. Christians increase one another's knowledge, strengthen one another's faith, clear one another's evidences. When the trees planted in God's orchard stand at a distance, and grow strange one to another, they are less fruitful.

(7) If you would be fruit-bearing trees, be *near the water of the sanctuary*: 'he shall be like a tree planted by the waters, and that spreadeth out the roots by the river; her leaf shall be green, nor shall it cease from yielding fruit' (Jeremiah 17:8). The Word preached will not only make us knowing Christians, but growing Christians. Ministers are compared to clouds (Isaiah 5:6); their doctrine drops as the rain, and makes the trees of God fruitful. I wonder not that they are barren trees and nigh unto cursing, that are not under the droppings of the sanctuary. A Christian can no more be fruitful without ordinances, than a tree without showers.

(8) And lastly, if you would fructify apace, *go to God and desire him to make you fruitful*; God is called the husbandman in John 15:1, and he hath an art above all other husbandmen. They can plant and prune trees, but if they be dead they cannot make them bear. God can make the barren tree bear, he can put life into a dead tree (Ephesians 2:5). It is not Paul's planting, but the Spirit's watering that must give the increase.

Pray to God to make you fruitful, even though it be by affliction; oftentimes God makes us grow in grace this way: 'No chastening for the present seemeth to be joyous, but grievous; nevertheless afterward it yieldeth the peaceable fruit of righteousness' (Hebrews 12:11).

The bleeding vine bears best. It is an observation that the pulling off some of the blossoms of a tree makes the fruit fairer; the reason is, because the sap hath the less to nourish; some writers say that they have known a tree by having too many blossoms hath blossomed itself dead. The notion holds true in a spiritual sense. God, by pulling off some of the blossoms of our comforts, makes us bring forth fairer fruit; for some have so blossomed in prosperity that they have blossomed themselves into hell. It is an ancient experiment that the planting some tender trees near the west sun doth them hurt, and parcheth the fruit, the sun being so extremely hot. Too much prosperity, like the west sun, doth Christians much hurt, and parcheth all good affections (Jeremiah 22:21).

O pray to God that he would make you fruitful, though it be by bleeding. Say, as Luther, Lord, wound where thou wilt, prune and cut me till I bleed, so that I may 'have my fruit unto holiness, and my end everlasting life' (Romans 6:22).